Sara Davies

with Alexandra Heminsley

We Can All Make It

THE SECRETS OF SUCCESS – MY STORY

PENGUIN BOOKS

TRANSWORLD PUBLISHERS
Penguin Random House, One Embassy Gardens,
8 Viaduct Gardens, London SW11 7BW
www.penguin.co.uk

Transworld is part of the Penguin Random House group of companies
whose addresses can be found at global.penguinrandomhouse.com

First published in Great Britain in 2022 by Bantam Press
an imprint of Transworld Publishers
Penguin paperback edition published 2023

A CIP catalogue record for this book
is available from the British Library.

ISBN 9781529177244

Typeset in Adobe Caslon by Jouve (UK), Milton Keynes.
Printed and bound in Great Britain by Clays Ltd, Elcograf S.p.A.

The authorized representative in the EEA is Penguin Random House Ireland,
Morrison Chambers, 32 Nassau Street, Dublin D02 YH68.

Penguin Random House is committed to a sustainable
future for our business, our readers and our planet. This book
is made from Forest Stewardship Council® certified paper.

1

What readers are saying about
We Can All Make It

'Sara writes as she speaks; the book flows
beautifully and her passion, wholeheartedness,
can-do approach and willingness for sheer hard
work are a total inspiration. Just love her!'

'The stories, [from] starting the business
to her Strictly journey, had me laughing,
crying and just generally feeling in awe of
this fabulous lady. An all-round inspirational
read. Couldn't put it down.'

'Down-to-earth, honest and inspiring. She is also a
wonderful ambassador for the North East of England,
and for women aspiring to go into business. A real
canny lass who is proud of her roots!'

'As a keen crafter for many years, it was great to
read Sara's story. It shows that with determination
you can achieve your dreams, and she certainly did.'

'Inspirational and educational. A must-read for
anyone interested in business.'

For Simon, who has always encouraged and empowered me to be the very best version of myself

Contents

We Can All Make It

Prologue

———

The cameras were ready, and so was I. But that didn't mean my heart wasn't pounding. Even my lucky shoes weren't calming me down. The shiny red-soled high heels I had finally bought myself after years of longing for them but being too stingy to fork out. Finally I was a Dragon, about to film my first ever series of *Dragons' Den*. I had made it far enough in business to become an investor, and now this was my opportunity to do it on the national stage, on one of the country's most beloved TV shows. A show I had watched since I was a kid. The dreams of future entrepreneurs were now in my hands. This was my chance to inspire the next generation of business leaders and have a whole lot of fun doing it. Take a deep breath, Sara. This is it.

When I was setting out in business, my battered old

copy of Duncan Bannatyne's memoir, *Anyone Can Do It*, held pride of place on my shelf. That I might get the chance to write one of my own seemed almost a dream too far back then. Almost. And now I was sitting on the same panel that had brought him to the public's attention and about to start work on my own book.

'Am I really here?' I wondered as I waited to see the first entrepreneur. It seemed unbelievable that I was ticking off such a huge life-goal already. It felt like only yesterday that I was behind the till at my parents' wallpaper and paint shop, helping out on a Saturday and dreaming of having a business of my own. But I was. And now, I want to show you how I got there – and beyond.

When I give talks and seminars, when I'm interviewed or even just out and about chatting, most people assume that there was some secret, some 'in', some leg-up in industry only they don't know about yet. Yes, I was lucky enough to have a supportive family who believed in me and my dreams, but what people don't seem to believe is that, beyond that, there is no magical secret behind my success.

For the whole of this journey, I have never thought of myself as anything but totally 'normal'. I haven't had any opportunities that were out of the ordinary. I went to an ordinary school, I grew up in an ordinary village and I had an ordinary childhood. When I first started being asked to talk about my 'path to success', I worried that it would be boring for people. Shouldn't I jazz it up a bit? Add some peril? Or a rich auntie along the way? Then I realized that wasn't the point. The point *was* that if I could do it, so can you.

People started to tell me that they felt empowered, knowing that I hadn't had anything but an ordinary start. It made them see that some of the roadblocks we think are in our way might not be real but only imagined. That we can be our own worst enemies if we don't believe that the opportunities often lie not just ahead of – or even behind – us, but within us.

I was ambitious from a young age. I don't remember ever seeing the point of doing something if I didn't give it absolutely my all. And I had parents who encouraged me from day one to be super-ambitious. They taught me that I could achieve anything if I put my mind to it. But what happened next was that I *did* put my mind to it.

Every chance I had, I worked really hard to take the little opportunities I saw and turn them into bigger ones in order to achieve my life goals. I spoke out when I wanted to try something. I never hesitated to learn more. And I asked for help when I needed it. But beyond that, my success is relatively simple: it comes from a lifetime of having big ambitions and setting my mind to achieving them.

I would love to say that there were some special secrets to my success. I could make a mint promising to tell them to you! But the reality is more inspiring and, hopefully, once you have read my story, you'll agree. Because what it boils down to is that if I can do it, so can you.

Chapter 1

Business in the Blood

———

Perhaps it is not so surprising that I grew up to be a businesswoman. We might not have had two pennies to rub together when I was a kid, but my dad really was king of the entrepreneurs. He bought a derelict old building on the high street of Coundon, a mining village in County Durham. Our whole life was then based there over the years – it became the headquarters for his many ventures, from double glazing to a bike shop, a dolls' furniture workshop, a transport company – even some mushroom growing – and much else along the way. And it was also our childhood home. My mam and dad still live there today.

Businesswise, my dad's mainstay was a property and transport courier company. He also set my mam and nana up with a wallpaper and paint shop. Well, I say 'shop', but they started out on the market, selling slight seconds and production overruns of wallpaper and all sorts, and gradually got more respectable as the years went by.

These family businesses weren't always massively successful, but they were always ours, and that meant that the whole family could make decisions about their careers *and* run the businesses in a way which also fitted in with the family. Working hours were compatible with school runs and summer holidays, and the businesses were the bedrock of family life: they evolved around us and we evolved around them. Most importantly, this meant that I was given a clear demonstration of the correlation between hard work and how we lived from the time I was a small child.

Having said that, when I was young, I'm not so sure any of the family thought I'd go into business. My dad is a traditional guy and was even more so when I was growing up, and I think that, having daughters, he hoped we would marry well as much as he hoped we'd have good jobs. If anything, we might help out in the shop with my mam and nana.

From the moment my mam was pregnant, Dad was saving for his babies – only he said it was to pay for private school for any boys or weddings for the girls. That was his mentality back then. So I think it took him by surprise when I started to take some interest in the wallpaper and paint shop – and how it worked as a business, not just as a Saturday job – when I was a young teenager, and started chipping in with ideas. But at that stage I wanted to be a teacher. I thought I was curious rather than ambitious, and helping out at the family business felt like helping out, not like learning a skill.

It was only when my GCSEs came round that I thought I would try Business Studies as a way to formalize what I was learning working in the shop. It felt like a no-brainer to me, as Business Studies just seemed like common sense, barely an actual subject. It was *real life*, not 'school stuff', wasn't it? In Maths and History you had to remember a ton of facts, but what we learned in Business Studies always seemed obvious to me. I used to ace the exams, which didn't feel like exams – I remember I even got 100 per cent in one of them.

I was taking such an interest in the family firm, and really finding a passion for it, so the next logical step seemed to be go to university and learn the theory behind business. It was around this time that I changed tack from wanting to train as a teacher to dreaming that I might return from university and take over the business, really knowing my stuff.

Business was in the blood. But the fact that I ended up studying the subject at York University and, from there, setting up my first business is also down to a few things that are decidedly less entrepreneurial, a little more romantic and, when it comes down to it, more a case of turning disadvantage into advantage.

When I was at school, I was a bit of a loner. I was I guess what you would call the geeky one – the opposite of all the girls in the cool crowd. I was more of a people-pleaser. I loved being the teacher's pet and thrived on praise. I also hated doing anything wrong – I just wanted to live by the rules!

I was in with the geeky crowd, the ones who studied really hard. I prided myself not on wearing cool make-up or trendy outfits but on reaching the top set in Maths. I certainly wasn't the cleverest kid in school; I wasn't really the best at anything. But I was an enthusiast – I tried it all! Swimming classes, gymnastics, badminton club. But I was clearly not *great* at anything, I just enjoyed trying it all out and doing my best. Despite my boundless enthusiasm and my mediocre results, it was sport that ended up being what brought me and my husband together.

While sport wasn't my thing, my dad was big into cricket, loved being able to support the local team and even taught me to be the scorer. This was how I met Simon. He was nineteen and had his own car, which seemed very cool to me and my mates. We were still only fifteen and didn't really know any guys who could drive. Before too long he offered to pick me up and give me a lift to the match. So I gave him my number and we did that for a bit, but after a while he called me when there was no match on and said, 'I was just wondering if you fancied a ride out, because I'm free tomorrow.'

'But there's no match on,' I said. 'Why would we have a ride out if there's no match on? I don't get it.'

He mumbled a bit about how he just thought it might be fun, so I agreed and, before I knew it, we were off playing tennis. I had no clue why we were doing this, but I found out later that he had seen me playing tennis once with my mates and had assumed I was really into it. Ha! I'm rubbish at tennis, but I was very excited about what seemed to be a really sophisticated date.

I borrowed a racket off the lad who lived next door and took the bus down to Bishop Auckland. I'd got myself a new T-shirt with 'Champion' written on it, because that was what I thought was the 'in' brand at the time. Simon realized within five minutes that I was terrible at tennis, and that this was going to be a very awkward date. But you know what? It wasn't. We ended up sitting at the side of the court chatting for ages, then went for a little walk. And he said, 'Do you want to have a ride out tomorrow too?'

We went out to the beach the next day and saw each other at the match the following Saturday. Only this time, while I was in the score box, all the other lads kept shouting, 'Eyes on the ball, Simon, not the score box!'

This was a lot to handle for me. I was not used to being an object of scrutiny and gossip, even on this small, local level. I felt like a laughing stock, and when

9

Simon came over and asked if I'd like to do anything after the match all I could say was, 'No. Just take me home, please.'

After that, he never did ask me out again. He just kept turning up in the wallpaper shop, appearing on a Saturday morning when I was at work, and next thing I knew, my gran was up in his face having a good look (my mam must have rung her!) to 'check him out': 'Is this him, Susan?' And to him: 'I hope you're looking after our girl.'

But he stuck it out, and I liked that. What I didn't like was being the subject of gossip at school. If one of the popular girls at school even walked towards me in a corridor I would get the shakes, thinking, 'Oh my god, she's gonna talk to me, she's gonna talk to me! What do I say?'

Eventually one of them came up to me and asked, 'Is it true that you've got a boyfriend who's twenty-five?'

'No, he's nineteen,' I replied. But you know how rumours can escalate as they make their way around a secondary school. I was mortified.

Had I brought any random nineteen-year-old boy home, my dad would probably have got the shotgun out. But because my parents had already kind of got to know him through the cricket and my mam had been scoping him out at the shop, they loved him. So, in the end, it didn't matter what the gossip around town was. My dad knew he was a good lad from a good family so, before I knew it, Simon had the lot of us twisted round his little finger.

Then there was the fact that my dad had been thirty-one when he got together with my mam, who was nineteen at the time, so he really was in no position to pile on the pressure. My grandparents hadn't approved of him at all – he was newly divorced, he had a variety of businesses, from a sweet shop to driving around selling cigarettes door to door – or ice creams in the summer, or pie and peas in the winter. And on top of that, my mam had dropped out of university after only three months to be with him instead of pursuing her studies. Her Catholic family were far from impressed, so I guess that's why my dad gave Simon an easier time of it. Especially when it came to my choices about university.

My goal when choosing where to do my degree was simply to find a course somewhere I could drive home from every weekend to see Simon – but also be just far enough away that it would justify the thousands of pounds my parents had saved and were now committed to spending to further my education. It was unspoken but assumed by then that when I came back from uni I would be taking over the family business, so I wanted to have a little bit of an adventure away from home. I wanted to spread my wings, and to have the university 'experience', but in such a way that I could have the home life I wanted with my boyfriend too.

When I got my GCSE results, I'd done okay. It was mostly Bs and Cs, but there were some As in there too. My A-level predicted results at the beginning of the year were two Bs and two Cs. But then I saw a course that really appealed at the University of York and realized that it would enable me to get the education I wanted without having to give up time with the man I loved. Perfect! However, there was a big but ... I needed three As to get in. My commitment to schoolwork ramped up significantly, even by my own already nerdy standards. I *had* to get that place. And it was starting to look like I would. But just as my predicted grades switched from Bs and Cs to straight As, I encountered an unexpected bump in the road: I had been working so hard, with such significant results, that my school suddenly wanted me to apply for Oxbridge. I was accidentally filtered above where I wanted to be and sent down south for entrance exams.

My god, I was so terrified I might actually get offered a place. I knew I would feel obliged to take it: people from my school never got into Oxford or Cambridge. My family would have expected me to take it, the teachers at the school too – everyone. So I didn't study for the exam and I didn't try hard. It feels terrible saying this, as I am going to go on about hard work so much for the rest of this book, but I guess if you really *don't* want something, it's hard to put in the hours. I really did not want the opportunity, and I would have felt terrible taking it when I knew so many other people did. But I would have disappointed so many more people if I had not taken it! I dodged the bullet, though – pretty much the only time in my life that not working as hard as I should have done actually paid off.

Instead, I stayed fixated on studying at York. Yes, it was a city, but it wasn't a big, scary city. And York was a small, campus-based uni – everybody knew everybody. I'm not a big-city girl and I'm not built for big-city life. The degree at York University was perfect: two years there, then a placement year and then a final year. And it was exactly the right sort of distance away from home for me.

This time I did put the hours in and, even though I had originally been predicted Bs and Cs for my A-levels, I did much better because it was the means to a life that I did want. The place was mine. And armed with the three As I had surprised everyone by getting, I had had first-hand experience of the relationship between some really hard work and some really great results.

I was so excited to arrive at my halls of residence that first day, because earlier in the year I'd been to visit a mate of mine who was studying at Newcastle University and she had the most wonderful room. The halls of residence were absolutely gorgeous, like Hogwarts. But my mam and dad pulled up outside my accommodation in York and it was full 1980s bleakness.

To make things worse, I was completely exhausted, as I had had the mad idea to take part in the Great

North Run that morning. I hadn't realized that the two things were going to be on the same day when I signed up to do it but, once I did realize, I was absolutely determined not to back out. My friend had persuaded me to join her doing it, telling me that it would be a great way to tone up before we started at university. 'We'll turn up to uni super-fit and stick thin!' she promised me, before ducking out on most of the training and then walking most of the way round.

Old Goody Two Shoes here did all the training and then ended up latching on to some other girl on the day, just to have someone to run with. She kind of dragged me round, and I was so proud of myself as we approached the finish line. I really did run most of it – half a marathon! – which was something I had never imagined I would be able to do. I had a vision of myself having a quick shower and arriving at university all dynamic and impressive, with my medal around my neck.

I did have my medal clanking around my neck when I turned up, but the rest of the vision never quite came true. When we arrived mid-afternoon there was no one around, and I could feel the nervous excitement draining out of me by the second, leaving me feeling flat and alone. Everyone else had clearly arrived first thing, unpacked and then gone off to start having fun. It was stupid little things that started to upset me, like there not being any space in the fridge for my stuff, there only being the cupboard that was out of reach for my pound-shop frying pan and packets of noodles.

My mam must have been quite nervous about it all too. I could see she was struggling with the idea of leaving me. It was written all over her face as she walked back to the car and my dad started the engine. Just as they were heading off, someone came by and mentioned that everyone was in the student union bar and that I should join them, and my dad was absolutely desperate to get Mam away before she started crying and set me off.

The course itself was quite elite; there were only thirty of us on it. And I had come from a very working-class background. I went to a run-of-the-mill school where, at the time, it wasn't common for students to go to the top universities. So, on the one hand, I didn't really fit in, and I knew it. But on the other hand, there was very little expectation on me. I had a chance to do better than anyone might have imagined, so I took the bait and pushed myself really hard through that first and second year, determined to prove that I was just as worthy of my place there as any of the rest of them.

I very much enjoyed what I was learning. And because it was such a practical course the tutors were the sort of people who had been there and done that and been successful somewhere. They weren't just teaching theory from a book, they had real-life experience, and I found this both fascinating and inspiring.

Some of the modules we did involved going into a business and assessing their problems and making recommendations directly to their management team. It felt like I was learning a lot of stuff right from the off, and I was trying to apply it quite often to the family business.

When we were in lectures I could hold my own, but in the halls of residence it was me and a lot of kids who had had a private education, and I often felt as if I stuck out like a sore thumb among them. There was one good friend I made called Rosie, who was more like me than any of the other girls in our halls of residence. She was from a pit village in Yorkshire and she was in a very similar situation to me in that she was doing everything on the cheap.

I was determined to try and live on a shoestring while I was there. I set myself the target of getting by on £10 a week, so I would drive a bunch of us up to the supermarket so we could buy as much stuff as possible in bulk and then just sort of scrape by on what we had. I don't know how I managed. I had bought my 'university kit' from the pound shop and got by with my one frying pan and my one saucepan. That was it. Every single meal I ate was either boiled or fried in one of those two pans, and then, instead of washing them up, I just used to rub around them with some kitchen roll so they looked clean. Disgusting! The cleaners would come round, and they were briefed to clean the kitchen but not our actual stuff, so they would wipe the surfaces around the pots and pans we had used then dump them all in a bucket on the floor. We used to call it the 'scum box'. And my stuff ended up in that scum box pretty much every day. I can't lie, there was an element of disarray to how I lived back then, but it was because that side of things was just not a priority to me – I was so absorbed by the course!

I had gone out and got a job working three nights a week at the local pub, so I didn't need to live quite this way, but I was still worried about my student loans all the time, and it was the degree I wanted, just as much as living it up and having a good time, so I just kept my head down and got on with it really.

The one extracurricular thing I got into was the ladies' cricket club. I knew how to play it from years of watching Simon, and I knew the rules and how to score, so I figured I would give it a go. As is so often my way, I was keen but pretty crap: I turned up to that damn women's cricket training every single week for months. Then, at the end of the first year, they were nominating the committee to run the team. There was the captain, the vice-captain and then the president. The captain and the vice-captain obviously have to be really good at cricket, but the president just runs the club. The president the year before had long ago sussed that I clearly didn't have an aptitude for the sport, but you couldn't fault my enthusiasm and how committed

I was to the club, so she had been mentoring me those last few months.

So I became the president of the cricket club in my second year, which is very unusual. Usually you kind of come through the ranks, and it's people in the third or fourth year who get that position. But my dogged enthusiasm and strong knowledge of cricket – plus the fact that it was the role with the least razzle-dazzle to it – meant the role was mine. And I basically took on running that ladies' club like a business. I set about writing a business plan and building a profit-and-loss and cashflow forecast, and quickly realized that to succeed we'd need money – so the first thing I did was to go out and get a sponsorship. The ladies' club had never been sponsored by anyone in the past (to be honest, they weren't performing at a level that could usually command any sponsorship), but the one thing I did have was the gift of the gab. I was able to talk my way into anything, so I struck a deal with a foreign kit company who gave us some cash and free kit in return for what I explained to them was very valuable advertising space.

I just totally bullshitted our way into those initial sponsors, because why not? What was the worst thing that would happen? The team would end up with no sponsor? They already had no sponsor! I promised the business that their name would be all over the kit and that we'd get them some great pictures, and I explained to them how well thought of they would become in the area because they had taken a chance on us. I really believed it – it was my first big sales pitch. And I was right.

Because with the sponsorship money we got, I paid for professional coaches for all the players, which meant the team got absolutely awesome within a pretty short amount of time. Next, I got seven of us on to a coaching course where we became qualified cricket coaches, and I coordinated us going into the local schools in the area to coach the kids. I wanted to make a bit of a positive difference, so we used to go and coach the kids so that they didn't see cricket as only a man's sport.

It was an unbelievable success: the team toured the country that year, playing in Stirling, at St Andrews – all over. We turned into a fantastic squad and became *the* club that people wanted to be in. I felt so proud that, even though I was just as crappy at cricket as I'd always been, I'd made that happen. Because I ran it like a business.

I was beginning to see that everything could be a business if you approached it with that sort of mentality, and I'm still like that today. Even if I'm just getting my nails done, I'll be asking the girl doing it, 'And are you renting a room here?' or 'Do you have to pay a commission on your sales?' and before long I'm giving her advice on how she can build a business. Half the time the girl couldn't care less – she just wants to paint people's nails nice colours in peace! But I'm always trying to work out how to take your business to the next level. I'm sure I drive some people round the bend, but I just can't help myself, in almost any situation, checking out the business angle.

I used to think it was the way I was wired, but now I wonder if it's more nurture than nature. Even if he didn't expect me to make anything of it in the early days, my dad brought me up to see life as one big entrepreneurial opportunity. He was the one explaining basic business terms to me at home over the breakfast cereal.

'Now, your turnover is how many sales you make, and that one's always the biggest number, pet. That's the one that people get excited about, the nice, big, shiny number. But you've got to remember your direct costs! That's what it costs to make your sales – how much does it cost you to make it or ship it? And that's what your gross profit is – your turnover minus your direct costs . . .'

For a lot of people, who didn't have a family business right there, who weren't going with their dad to buy the stock and who had never had that buzz of persuading someone to buy the wallpaper they knew would make the family business a bigger profit than the roll next to it, these terms might have been baffling or overwhelming. But I had an example, and one that I could touch and engage with for each of these lessons.

I *knew* that 'profit' was the word to get really excited about, that that was your turnover minus your direct costs and your indirect costs, the ones like wages or marketing which might fluctuate, and then your taxes. I learned those things alongside learning to ride my bike or use cutlery. He might not even have realized he was doing it, but my dad had given me the space to learn about business from the ground up. He just wanted me to be the very best version of me; he didn't care if it came with an Oxbridge polish if the experience was solid. And with him, it was.

I think this might have been something my fellow students had not banked on. But their fancy education and their sense of self made me more determined to do well at university, to get the very best from it. I decided to show everyone what I was worth: by the end of my second year, I was the highest-achieving student on the course, number one out of all thirty of us. And that gave me the incentive to work all the harder and do all the better.

I had seen now that if I had something to aim for and I put in the work, it really was possible to be the best. I had worked out what I needed to do to get to the top. Most of the time, the answer was just 'work as hard as you can', but a lot of it was that solid business grounding I had had at home. When I look back to try and pinpoint an early formative moment in my business life, it was my experience of that first year and the boost I felt when I realized that I could do it, silver spoon or no silver spoon.

Chapter 2

You've Got to be Shitting Me, Pet

I had known it was coming a while, and I knew what a lot of my fellow students were going to do, but I still didn't have the highest of hopes for my placement year at university. Most of my coursemates were London-bound to do 'proper' placements in junior management roles, but there was no way a country bumpkin like me was going to be heading down to the capital for a whole year, so I set about finding a business nearby that I could try and get some experience in.

In the end it was Simon's mum who found some-where for me. Simon's parents had a painter and decorator, a little old man called Derek. And I don't say that lightly, he really was a little old man. He should have retired years ago, but he was a friend of the family and still did bits for my future in-laws, Val and John.

And his son Adrian was married to a lady called Glenda who had set up her own business, which was actually doing quite well. Or at least that was how it seemed.

Adrian, by all accounts, was a very, very successful person who worked in IT and was earning a big salary. Glenda was also very successful in the business, and in fact that is how they met. But she was an artist on the side, and crafting in the mid-2000s was going through a massive boom. It was before the recession, a period of huge economic prosperity anyway, and little craft businesses were opening up left, right and centre. And doing well!

Added to this, Glenda really was a fantastic artist, so what she'd done was to open her own business selling rubber stamps of her designs. Now, if you're not into card-making, this might not mean much to you – you might just think that rubber stamps are something that kids play with, a dinosaur here or a unicorn there. One step up from potato printing. But in the craft world, and in making greetings cards in particular, they are a big deal – especially ones as beautiful as Glenda's were.

What she did was hand-draw stunning designs, the sort of thing that would look gorgeous on a card for a loved one, and then converted the drawing into a rubber stamp which other people could then ink up, stamp on to their card and then maybe colour in or personalize. These days, things like that tend to be made of acrylic, but back then she had her own vulcanizing machine.

She would get her designs converted on to matrix boards and they would melt the rubber on to the board and that would create a rubber stamp which would be mounted on to a little piece of foam and then a block. It was huge in the industry at the time, and hers were real showstoppers.

At first, it was just going to be a summer job, between my first and second year. I was there for three months, and I did a bit of everything. I used to operate the vulcanizer, cut the rubber stamps out, help pack orders – whatever needed doing. We were a tiny little team of just a couple of people, so you'd just do anything. And the business was doing really, really well.

By the end of the summer, Glenda asked me, 'Why don't you come and do that full year's placement here?' She was offering £1,000 per month – which was half of what some of my coursemates were getting down in London. But, because I wanted to stay close to home, I said yes.

By the time I had completed my second year at university nine months later, the business, which was called Graphicus, had grown enormously. When I came back, Glenda had a PA/office manager, a company car – the works. The business really did look like it had taken off. As I walked in that first day back, checking out the massive fountain in the forecourt, the enormous bright blue Subaru she was driving, all the office furniture from Barker & Stonehouse, I was so impressed.

'Wow, she's done really well,' I thought. 'She'd just started the business, and now it's taken off like this.'

A moment or two later she was introducing me to all these new staff, giving it the full 'This is Paul, he runs accounts. This is Caroline, she's my PA and office manager' and so on. I felt like I'd arrived at Downton Abbey, with all the staff lined up outside the big house – there were eight or ten of them now!

But . . . there was a small part of me wondering what all these people actually did. So I decided that for my first week I was going to start with accounts. I had just done a big module about accounts at university and I was hungry to put it all into action as I could see that the company not only had an internal accountant but was also sending a lot of the more complicated work to an accountant outside the business.

When I worked for them that first summer I'd been in jeans and a jumper, helping out with more manual tasks. Basically, I'd been a glorified box-packer. But now I was an office worker with a desk, and I was determined to make that point before I started delving into the accounts. I didn't have any cash myself, though, so I remember a couple of days before I started Simon took me out and bought me a pair of Ted Baker trousers. I had never owned anything so fancy in my life! And for a long time they were the only thing that fancy I did have. I wore them most days, with a variety of blouses, and I still have them somewhere.

It was the start of a habit of mine, where I always try and wear something appropriate to how I want people to feel about me. At Graphicus, I wanted to have that position of authority. I was younger than everybody else and I knew I was at the bottom of the rung in terms of getting paid. What I wanted was respect for my position, for me to be clearly differentiated from the people who were packing the orders in their casual gear. I wanted it to look like I was the one managing strategy, and for people to respond accordingly.

'Right,' I told Glenda. 'I'm going to go through all of your accounts. And I'm going to see what we can save having to send to the outside accountant because *I'll* be able to do it now.'

The first thing I had to do was familiarize myself with their accounting software, Sage, but before long I had made a start on tracking what money we had in what accounts, and reconciling it all so that I could see what was showing in the system and where we could tighten things up. But when I had finished there was a shortfall. I couldn't track it at all, and I was thinking, 'Have I not been told about the American sales? Have I not been told the password for some other account? Where is it?'

I didn't want to lose face in front of Glenda in my first week, so first of all I had a word with Caroline, trying to figure out what I was missing. She just said, 'Well, Adrian sometimes has to pay the wages at the end of the month if we're a bit short.'

'I'm sorry, what?' This turn of events had most definitely *not* been covered in my course.

'Yeah,' she said, and I wasn't sure if she thought this was normal or not. 'When I go to pay the wages, if there's not enough money in the bank account, I'm to tell Adrian, and then he gives me the money.'

At this point I realized I had to go in and see Glenda, because things were not making sense. They were doing so well! But they sometimes didn't have enough money for salaries at the end of the month?

'Glenda,' I said, trying to sound as grown-up and businesslike as possible, 'where's this extra money coming from? Because I can't do the year-end accounts if I can't account for it.'

That's when it all came out.

'We've got all this money on credit cards,' she explained. 'Sometimes we don't even have the money for wages between us, so we've been putting it on credit so we don't have to lay anyone off . . .'

'Oh my god! Why the hell have you hired me then? You can't afford another wage . . .' was the first thing I said. 'I'm probably the cheapest wage in the building, but you still can't afford another grand a month.'

She looked at me, and I felt so sorry for her when she said in a tiny voice, 'I kind of thought you might be able to help?'

It was June at the time. I had literally just finished my second year. So I thought, 'Let's give it a go. If it all goes belly up by September, I'll just go back to university, start the third year and graduate without the placement year.' I really had nothing to lose by giving it a try for a few weeks, as I was still living at home, I wasn't earning much anyway, and I guess I thought I might learn something – even if it was what *not* to do.

I was absolutely mortified for Glenda because I could see how upset she was, and there was no doubt that she was such a talented artist – she still is. And this is the problem with our industry. The craft world is full of people who are massively talented, whether it's in art or craft or whatever. They are so passionate about the industry, but they sometimes don't have enough of the fundamental business building blocks that you need to get a company really working well. And back when this was happening it was a period of economic prosperity – it was almost like money was growing on trees. These little craft shops were opening up every week, all over the country – how could you *not* make money? But as I now realized, it's not just about making the sales – it's about controlling the costs and the overheads to run the company as a profitable entity.

These were highly intelligent people – but it's not about intelligence. Glenda was probably more intelligent than I was, but because I had grown up in a business environment (even a small-scale one!) I saw it differently. My parents were born entrepreneurs, not that I would have even called it that as a child – it seemed like way too much of a big fancy word. I would probably have just said, 'They run their own business.' But they *were* entrepreneurs, they had been working for themselves successfully for twenty years by this point, and I had understood since the first day I helped them out as a child that *it's never just about making sales.*

My dad could tell you every supplier where we bought every roll of wallpaper in our shop, and how much he paid for it. He could tell you how much profit we were making on each one, and made sure I knew it too. People would come into the shop to buy some wallpaper and I'd think, 'I'm going to sell them this one because we make more profit on this one.'

It was an instinct instilled in me from my very first Saturday job behind the till. I learned so early on to look at everything from a profit perspective rather than just the thrill of a sale – almost before I'd even realized I'd learned it. But it was clearly a lesson that Glenda was still learning. There's that age-old saying, 'Turnover is vanity, profit is sanity', and Graphicus was the very definition of this not happening.

They were making more and more sales every month, yet Glenda wasn't making money. She had all these sales, yet when she got to the end of the month there wasn't always enough money in the account to clear the wages. So they'd get out a credit card. There must be so many people like this who have gone through the same thing – not just in our industry, but in *any* industry.

I just felt so overwhelmingly sorry for her, and I really wanted to help. I thought, 'Oh my god, Glenda, you must have been going through hell the last few weeks and months.' She had all these staff depending on her for their mortgages and the costs were ballooning. She really needed help.

She asked me to go and meet the accountant, to have a chat with him and talk through a potential plan for the business. She also wanted me to meet the bank manager. I went along with it, but I was so nervous – one woman with a head full of magic and half a degree in a room with this guy with a stern face in his grey suit. I was trying to sound professional, using all the 'official' terms I had learned at university, but what I think actually swung it was that I talked sense about my parents' business. I was able to say with conviction that we were making that successful, and to explain why. Unlike the bits of the meeting when I sounded like I'd swallowed my textbook, going on about 'wrapping our arms around the cost base and the profitability'.

I had nothing to lose. Literally! So we gave it a go.

The plan to fix the business was one of two halves. In short, we had to cut costs in half and double sales. So I had two separate plans: one for the costs, one for the sales.

The first thing was that half the staff had to go. Lovely Paul in accounts was first, and I was distraught. But if I was going to do the job I'd said I would, I had to be the one to tell Glenda, 'We can't afford to pay his wages.' Bearing in mind that his mam was working there too, it was a really difficult day. Especially as everyone in the building must have known it was me, as I was the one suddenly saying that not a penny in the business could be spent without it going through me. I had even created a form that had to be signed each time business cash was spent, and it had to be signed by me, not Glenda.

'This only works if it comes from the top,' I told her. 'Every single person – including you and Adrian – have to fill in one of these if you need to spend out on something.'

And sure enough, before long I was signing her form to say that she could put petrol in her bright blue Subaru if she was driving it to work. I was making her think. About every single penny. The fancy office furniture stopped coming. We no longer had a stationery cupboard that was full of crap. We no longer used the photocopier at 10p a sheet. I stopped it all. I plugged the leaky bucket of spending.

As for the sales side of things, I had all sorts of ideas. First, I sorted out their website. Bearing in mind this was 2005, no websites were that good, but the Graphicus one really was rubbish. It was written in something called Dreamweaver, an Adobe program, and I worked out that you could go online and watch easy tutorials on how to work it. The way it operated was not that dissimilar to Microsoft Word or PowerPoint – if you knew the basics of those, you could master the tables and the format. So I basically redesigned the website in this program over a couple of weeks to try and get the web sales up. I'm not saying it was as beautiful as Glenda's art, but it did make it clear that you could buy the products from us and what they were.

Next up, I could see that one basic task that needed doing was to get more shops selling our products. So I started going through the backs of the craft magazines and turned myself into a self-appointed sales rep. I was ringing up the craft shops and trying to convince them to take our products day after day, and after a while I was opening quite a few new accounts. Within a couple of months, we went from having our stock sold in a couple of dozen stores to nearly two hundred shops stocking our products. This was all over the country, because there were new shops opening practically every week and they'd all be taking a £10 advert in the back of *Crafts* magazine or wherever, because online sales weren't that big back then.

I was driving all over, having discovered that I could go out and do a little tour around half a dozen shops and take six orders while I was out. One day, after driving to Newcastle and placing a £1,000 order, I asked Glenda if I could be paid some sales commission to top up my wages – after all, so far as I understood it, that's how sales reps in other industries worked. And, essentially, being a sales rep was now firmly within the job remit!

She said that she would think about it, but that commission never made its way to me. Which irked, because I was still the lowest-paid member of staff on the team, but I was working so hard. I let it slide for now, as I knew we still had to turn things around.

The third thing I did was to up the profile of Graphicus at consumer shows, which were, and still are, massive in the industry. There were consumer shows on every weekend, across the country. They had names like the Big Stamping and Scrapbooking Show, and some were huge, in places like the NEC or Alexandra Palace, but others were in the likes of Stevenage Leisure Centre. You could go and see the latest products, watch them being demonstrated, maybe even try things out – and Graphicus's products were perfect for this.

By now I was managing the cashflow for the company – watching what sales were coming in from the shops, what the website was making, what it was all costing us, and so on. So if it got to the middle of the month and we were short on cash, I would suggest we should go out and do a consumer show. You could sell three or four grands' worth of product in a weekend, the cash impact was immediate and it was all product that we had in stock so the cost to the business was minimal.

I used to unpack the shop into the back of my dad's

big yellow van, which he'd hire to us for fifty quid, drive to wherever a show was on, and sell whatever I could. One Friday I said to Caroline, the office manager, 'You, me and the stock – Stevenage Leisure Centre this weekend?' And she was like, 'Eerrrr . . .'

'But we can't pay the bills otherwise . . .' I had to explain. 'And I can't do it on my own.'

She knew she was going to be out of a job if my plans didn't work, so this poor woman who barely knew me was in the van before she'd had a chance to realize what she'd signed up for. I think it was only once we were on the road that I told her we didn't have the budget for two hotel rooms. But we did it, you know. We worked hard all weekend, and we'd come home with three or four grand.

Now, I didn't mind doing this. The environment I had been brought up in meant that I was far from afraid of hard work. Especially when you were getting results like this. But there was one thing I resented so much. I would drive home on a Sunday night, exhausted after working all weekend and knowing I'd still be in on time on Monday, and when we got to the offices Glenda would be there but didn't help us unload the van.

I remember thinking, 'So I'm trailing my sorry ass the length and breadth of the country at the weekend for your company, and you don't even want to help us unload the van?'

Perhaps she had her reasons, and other, more pressing things to do, but the feeling of not being properly appreciated stuck with me for ever. The minute I started my own company I knew that I never, ever wanted my staff to feel about me the way I felt about her in those moments. It has guided the way I've tried to behave with my staff ever since – even down to the fact that I wore jeans in the office for years, just so that the people working for me knew I was ready to roll up my sleeves and get the work done, it didn't matter who you were. It's all well and good having your Ted Baker trousers for a meeting with the bank, but they're not all you need, and nor should they be.

It wasn't all hard work and resentment, though, because it was at these consumer shows that I discovered the people who were to become my tribe for the next fifteen-plus years – the crafters. I learned who the people who really love card-making are, I learned how the craft itself worked and I learned what they wanted.

The main thing I discovered was that they want to learn. Crafters want to improve, to expand their skills, to try new things. And the best way for them to do this is to watch demonstrations. So if Glenda had drawn a beautiful flower stamp, I had to have a card made with that flower stamp on display, and I'd be, 'Look, you can make this, loads of times, with this stamp, and it's only £4.99!'

Then I realized that if you have things that you can

demonstrate, people will stop at your stand to watch the demonstrations, so I had to teach myself to use the products, and use them well enough to make them look exciting but not so well that I looked distant, too professional, making something that 'normal' folk could never manage to make. I would never have been good enough to be a pro, but I could do 'just good enough' really well. So I'd have the example that a pro had done on display, and then I'd do one alongside it, showing how an ordinary Joe could make a card look great if they had the right tools. And in the act of doing this, I learned about the sensory pleasure of crafting, how relaxing it could be and how fantastic the sense of achievement is when you create something lovely for someone you care about.

Quickly, it became clear that people would buy either because of a demonstration or because of a deal. So if I bundled the two together, put on a demonstration and then said, 'You can buy everything I've just used and save an extra tenner. Right now,' suddenly they had a reason to buy here and buy now. What I didn't know while I was learning this was that these were also the fundamental underpinnings of TV shopping: people buy from people.

When we were at the consumer shows, the demonstrators who drew the biggest crowds were usually the ones who were on the shopping-TV channels. They were like mini-celebrities in the crafting world, and it quickly became obvious that as Glenda was a really good demonstrator as well as such a great artist, I should be trying to get her on one of these channels too.

So I got on the phone to Ideal World, one of the channels which did a lot of craft stuff, and eventually I got her a booking. By now I was so used to selling her products into the buyers in shops and to the crafters at the shows that I had a great pitch, and they took an appearance from her. I was thrilled, because if your products are on TV, then you can also ring up the shops and say, 'Listen up, we've got a new range launching and it's going to be on TV next Saturday, so do you want to have some stock for your shop?' So you were kind of selling twice – to the people buying via the TV channel and to the shops, which were excited to have a product that they could say was on TV.

The only stumbling-block was that I needed Glenda to do the shows. She was now being asked to go from Barnard Castle to the Ideal World studios in Peterborough, to stay overnight and then do a broadcast showing how to use her products. It was a lot of time away from home, but the TV channel were really pleased with the sales and they were wanting her to go every month. So I offered to go and do the shows she didn't want to do. I made no secret about how I didn't know how to craft to anything like her standards, but wasn't the whole point of the products that absolutely anyone could create something beautiful at home with them? Might using me even work *better*?

Within three months of my starting at Graphicus we'd got the business to a point where it had gone from being in the red to it now all of a sudden making a profit every single month. My plan had got us debt-free, profitable every month and on an even keel.

I think that for those first three months Glenda could see the massive impact I was having, and that I was reversing a bad situation. When the bank manager came around he told us he was comfortable with the business and that we didn't need careful watching any more. And Glenda's response to him was: 'It is all her doing.' She really did acknowledge that it had been me and my strategy that had turned things around, and I remember feeling a million dollars because she'd said it out loud.

What Glenda probably had not banked on was that I was prepared to do whatever it took to get this business working, not just out of dire straits for a month or two, but properly turned around for the long term. And if that meant learning how to craft and present live on TV, then so be it. It wasn't that I was interested in going on TV at all. But off I trotted to Peterborough . . .

I approached the TV work the same way I had approached my demonstrations at the shows. I introduced myself as an amateur and stuck to that.

'I work for Graphicus, and Glenda is this incredibly

talented designer whose company it is. We are so lucky to have her stamps, as I can't draw for toffee. But look, Glenda drew this, and now all I do is ink it up and stamp it and colour it in, and look! I've got a card that looks really awesome. I'm absolutely hopeless at drawing, and this is so much more effective . . .'

I think it was the humility and the accessibility that worked. No, I didn't have the credibility of being the artist, but I made it a little bit more human and more real. I had done so many consumer shows I knew what it was that made the customer tick. I knew which demonstrations worked, which buttons to push and what keywords to use. I knew what was going to create a sale when I was live in front of people, and I worked out that I could just take that and apply it to being in front of the camera. Just as you can see an audience's ears prick up, see people lean in when you get to the good bit, so you could see the sales coming in when you were broadcasting live. And I absolutely loved it.

I knew I loved the business too. I loved the people, the crafters, the shops I was selling into – the lot. Back then I had no intention of starting my own business in the industry. I had been thinking I would probably graduate, come home and take over the family wallpaper and paint shop. But now I was starting to talk to Glenda about life after graduation. There were quite a few things I did that nobody else would have the skills to do, and she wouldn't be able to pay them to do. But there was a new accounts woman coming in, and a sales agent, and she said she wasn't sure that they could afford me as well as these two new staff members.

'I appreciate that you've worked hard for the business the last year,' she said, raising my hopes a little. 'So if you wanted to keep working for us, I could give you some production work.'

And she offered me minimum wage cutting rubber stamps for her. What did I think?

'You've got to be shitting me, pet' was what I thought. And I told her no thank you and headed back to university for my final year.

For my leaving present, she gave me a pen. It wasn't a Montblanc – not that I even knew what they were back then – or even a fifteen-quid Parker pen. No, no, it was one of the ones where you click the four nibs down for the four different colours. She gave me that and a fancy notebook to take notes in at university.

As I left the building that final time, I remember seeing that and thinking, 'Well, I never got the bloody commission. All I got was this multicoloured pen and a notebook.' Except that wasn't all I got. It was *all she gave me*, but I had come away with the bigger prize: I had found my industry, and I had had my first idea for a product.

Chapter 3

I Could Sell
a Ton of Those

There was one question that kept coming back to me whenever I demonstrated Graphicus products at the consumer shows. It seemed so obvious. But it also seemed that no one was answering it.

'Do you sell an envelope to go with that card?'

How was no one doing this? The cards were getting better and better, more ornate and more popular – but there didn't seem to be anyone who had thought that what goes around the cards is just as important as the card. And it seemed pretty clear to me that if I could provide a solution to that problem, I could have a product of my own to sell at the shows, and perhaps even on TV.

One product that was already out there in the market was folding pieces of board: wooden or plastic boards with various grooves so you could score out various sizes of card to make either boxes or greetings cards. Glenda sold the ones for making cards, and my engineering brain, which was already used to thinking about the best way to fit paper around certain shapes (even if it was wallpaper and people's living rooms!), had always preferred demonstrating those at the shows to demonstrating some of the more artsy stuff.

I was never quite sure how convincing I was with the frillier end of things, but there was a certain satisfaction in getting the card to bend perfectly, exactly where you wanted it to, and if I wanted a boost, I'd often think to myself at the start of a show, 'Right, I'm going to sell an absolute ton of those card-making boards today.' And I'd sit and show people how to fold cards for hours. Meanwhile, no one was making envelopes, and where was the fun in just having a pack of them for sale at the side of your stand?

The only possible solution I could find to the problem was templates. You'd just draw around them then fold them into the size you wanted, but you weren't going to get that crisp edge you did with the folding boards, plus you needed one template for every size of envelope. So I brought all the bits I had amassed home, showed them to my dad and said, 'Everybody likes these folding boards, and you can only buy templates for envelopes. Can we think of a way to bring the templates *into* a folding board?' So we worked on it for a few months, my dad and I in the garage, trying out different set-ups with the odds and ends from the box where he kept all his pieces of wood – then he chatted to his engineering mates at the local joiner's about all sorts of ways we could make it better.

He'd bring one in and I'd be like, 'That doesn't work, Dad,' over and over again, until we finally figured out one that did work. The minute we eventually stumbled on a folding-board style that actually worked to make an envelope, I thought, 'My god, this is so simple. How has nobody ever thought of this before?'

I now know that all the best ideas usually are like that – you barely need to 'invent' them, you just have to find a way to make the product you really need to solve a genuine problem that people have. The penny drops in your mind. And the minute it did, my dad knew what had to come next.

'You have to get yourself a patent for it, pet.'

I had no idea how to go about getting a patent. This was 2005 and I was still in my third year of university. They either hadn't got to that bit on the course, or they weren't going to, so it was down to me to find out. There was a government-run service called Business Link at the time. I had read about them before on one of the courses I did, about how they helped local businesses with advice, so it seemed like a good place to start.

It had been set up by Michael Heseltine MP over

ten years before, and it was there specifically to support up-and-coming businesses, to try and grow the next generation of entrepreneurs. So I contacted them, saying that I really needed some help, and I was assigned a Business Personal Adviser. He was called Richard Hall, and he is still someone I keep in touch with to this day. I could not have been treated better or received better advice from him. He was able to walk me through setting up a company, choosing a name (I went with Crafter's Companion, because that is what I wanted to be – a companion to any crafter) and the application for my first patent. And thank god he did, because I have since seen many entrepreneurs in *Dragons' Den* who have clearly misunderstood the process, at great cost to themselves or their business.

How it works is that you have to apply for the patent before you tell *anybody* about the idea. And it only costs £500 to submit your initial basic idea. Once the patent office acknowledges receipt of your application, this is known as your filing date. The application doesn't have to be too detailed, you just submit your idea to the patent office, pay your £500 and, at that point, you have twelve months until what's called a priority date to go out and assess whether or not it's a good idea and whether or not you want to spend thousands of pounds on a formally written patent application. But if you don't get that first filing date nailed down, and you show people your idea, asking for advice, going on

Dragons' Den, whatever – technically, there's no proof that you had that idea first. And that is where a *lot* of people trip up.

Once that initial part of the process was secured, Richard introduced me to different patent lawyers who could help with the next stage, as well as some different IP people. These are people who look after your IP (intellectual property), which, when you're designing a product that you're pretty sure no one else has come up with yet, is really very important. And if you can hold on for a couple of chapters, you're going to find out just how important.

Richard even helped me to look at various manufacturing options and get quotes. It really was an incredible resource, and it allowed me to meet people who could help me on my journey to my first business. Knowing that it was government funded gave me that extra confidence, because I wasn't worried that Richard had an agenda or a financial incentive to lead me in any one direction. He wasn't just some shady guy I'd met at a conference going, 'Nah, you need to talk to my mate Dave,' or whatever.

Instead, he was simply someone who came along to every meeting to lend an extra listening ear. He helped me to sort through what I had got out of each meeting afterwards, asking what I'd liked, what I needed, what made sense and all the rest of it. I didn't need a loan or a grant, but I did need someone who could point me in the right direction with all that sort of stuff, and he really did that.

These days, Business Link doesn't exist; it was disbanded a few years later, as often happens. But we did invite Richard to Crafter's Companion's tenth-birthday celebrations a few years back, and he was absolutely made up and blown away by how far we'd come since those early days. It was brilliant to see him!

Back then, it all felt very grown up, very quickly. The Ted Baker trousers were getting another good wearing, and I was desperate to be taken seriously because I knew my idea was good and I was certain that there was a market for it. The next thing I had to do was to get in touch with Ideal World, as I knew from my experience at Graphicus that if I really wanted sales, they held the keys to the kingdom.

The minute I knew we could go into production I gave my old contact there a call, explaining that I had a business idea and I wanted to pitch it myself.

'When can I come down and tell you all about it?' I asked.

'Oh, we thought you had left Graphicus and gone back to university,' they said.

'Well, I have. I'm still there. But I really want to pitch this to you, I think Pam's going to love it . . .'

Of course, I was hoping Pam would love it. Pam was Pam Kershaw, the buyer for Ideal World and the woman who had access to hundreds of thousands of wallets.

And could open them for me if she booked me and my product – which was by now called the Enveloper – on to the show.

The woman is about fifteen years older than me, always wears black – lots of drapey, flowing black – and seems so lovely. She smiles during your meetings, and the words she uses make it sound as if she's your best friend. But there's a steely edge. As I learned to my cost.

So I could not believe it when little old optimistic me turned up, pitched the Enveloper to her in person, and she beamed back, saying, 'Oh, this is such a wonderful idea, Sara. Congratulations.'

Fantastic!

'Right then,' she continued. 'We can make this a Pick of the Day. And for such a fantastic product we'll need to order eight thousand units.'

Amazing!

Being Pick of the Day meant that the Enveloper would be the main deal of the day – have tons of airtime and the best possible introduction to the market. I was so proud, and so excited. I literally left the offices and air-punched till my arm ached. 'I've nailed it!' I thought. 'I've got my opening order, and *what* an opening order it is.' Eight thousand units at £3.30 was a lot of money, after all.

But after that I could never get hold of her. She just never followed up with us. Still, I had a date. I understood her to have said in a formal meeting, on her business premises, that she wanted eight thousand units. So I went off and made eight thousand units.

We didn't have a very long time to get this initial order made, and I had no cash at all in the bank to pay a manufacturer to make the product. So, obviously, I got the family roped in again. My dad, as is often the case, had a plan.

He had been running his own businesses for forty years by now, and he was the master of finding inventive ways around cashflow. Back when he had market stalls, he would drive to Manchester on a Friday night, buy whatever stock he needed with a cheque – knowing full well that it couldn't be cashed until the Monday because the banks were closed over the weekend. He'd spend the whole weekend working hard on the stall to sell all the stock and then rush to the bank first thing Monday and deposit the cash, ready to cover the cheque he'd written three days earlier. The bank wouldn't lend him money, so he used to do this. And he decided we needed to try a version of the same – as well as using his excellent contacts – with the Enveloper.

We found some local joiners, and Dad persuaded them to take on the work – well, they were actually window-makers, but they had the same skills and used the same sort of materials and the same machines for routing the lines that were needed for the Enveloper, so we persuaded them to help us out. You should have heard my dad!

'Now, Tony, this is gonna be the biggest contract you've had in your life, mate. You know they've ordered eight thousand, don't you? I mean, look how big the company is! It's on that TV channel! A slam dunk. You are guaranteed you're gonna get paid for it. But, mate, it's forty-five-day terms. So we'll write you the cheque now, like *today*. But just don't cash it until we get ours in forty-five days . . .'

Now that's the gift of the gab. I guess it's where I got it from.

To be fair, my dad had been buying windows from Tony for years. I wouldn't say they were best friends or anything, but they were good business mates. And my dad is just so good at walking into a room and commanding the mood, telling people, 'This is how it's gonna be,' but doing it in a way that makes them think they are fine with it. It's not even that they're just fine with it – half the time he manages to sell them the dream that it's the biggest business opportunity of their life.

'Of course this is what you're going to do. And I'm going to make this happen for you. Isn't that wonderful?'

That is very much his vibe. So poor old Tony probably left that meeting feeling a little bit as if his head had been caught in a whirlwind, but feeling good all the same. I don't doubt that he came away thinking, 'Oh, yeah, I've got this big new contract today,' and not 'Oh my god, I might not get paid for these things. What am I doing?'

I was back at university by this point, and the joiners were in our village, so my dad would go there every night and pick up however many Envelopers Tony and the crew had made that day. They would be covered in sawdust because of the slicing of the MDF boards to create the grooves, so I paid my sister five pence per unit to sit with the hairdryer and blow off all the sawdust. I had also got some transparent stickers printed with the letters A, B, C, D, E, F on the top to indicate the various envelope sizes, so I got her to stick them on too, and pack each Enveloper into a bag with an instruction sheet I'd typed out and then photocopied on how the product worked.

She'd do it when she got in from school, a couple of hundred a night! She was only fifteen. But it was all hands on deck if we were going to get to eight thousand units in time for the show. Dad was storing them in the garage until we had them all finished, and then he was going to drive them down. It was a lot of work, for everyone. But we got there.

The day Dad said they were all ready to be delivered to Ideal World he called me and said, 'Right, kid, usually when I do deliveries, they need to be booked in at the warehouse.' So I called the warehouse.

'I've got some Envelopers for delivery for the show on the 24th of October . . .'

'Right,' said the guy in the warehouse. 'Just let me know your purchase order number and I'll book it in for you.'

'Oooh, I haven't got it,' I replied. 'Can you get it off Pam Kershaw?'

'No, I'm not getting it off Pam Kershaw,' came back the perfectly reasonable reply. 'You'll have to get it off Pam Kershaw. Get the purchase order and ring back, and then we can book it into the warehouse.'

So I reached out to Pam – a few times – and, finally, she got back to me.

'Hiya, Sara,' she said, her voice full of smiles. 'So we've decided we definitely do want the product, but we think it's not really the level for a Pick of the Day – so we just want it as an upsell now. So I'll write you the purchase order now, but we don't need eight thousand. I'll cut the PO for fifteen hundred …'

The floor felt as if it had just dropped from beneath me. The difference between being an upsell and being Pick of the Day is that instead of being the focus of the show and essentially having an hour to demonstrate your product eight times over the course of the day, you just have a few minutes at the end of the show, after they've focused on whatever the Pick of the Day is. So, obviously, they're not expecting you to do big money because you've only got five minutes. Which means they order stock accordingly.

I was devastated. All I could think of was that cheque we had given Tony. I was selling the Envelopers to

Ideal World for £3.30 per unit, making a pound profit on each one and paying Tony and his team £2.30 for each unit. Even if I made no profit at all and sold the whole fifteen hundred that Pam was now ordering, there was no way that would cover what we owed Tony. Which was £18,400. At best, we were going to be able to give him £4,950. Which was *quite* the shortfall.

I felt sick to my stomach. Terrified by how much I had put on the line, and all because I was too naive to know that I needed to get a purchase order before I started playing the big I Am, asking the whole family for help and cutting cheques I did not have the confirmed orders to cover.

My mind was racing, trying to work out how I could cover what I now owed, and to such a short and specific deadline. Even if I sold my car, that would only bring in a couple of grand. Even if my dad sold his car, it probably wouldn't cover it. Every time I closed my eyes at night, all I saw was that massive thirteen and a half grand flashing up. Taunting me.

My family was amazing, though. Even if they were all furious and panicking, they never showed it, not even for a minute. But I was absolutely filled with internal panic. I'll work all hours if needs be, I know I can sell to almost anyone if they're in front of me, and I was convinced that the Enveloper was a great product. This time, however, I had no solution. Nothing. Just a head full of dreams and a heart full of fear.

One good thing about this was that I barely had a chance to worry about presenting the product on TV. I had done short sections on Ideal World before, and now that I didn't have a show to myself, I put any anxieties about my performance to the back of my mind and tried to focus on ways to pay that cheque. Having said that, I did vomit in the green room toilet almost the minute I arrived. It wasn't performance anxiety, it was that damn thirteen and a half grand still whirling through my mind.

The panic wasn't just making me sick – it was stopping me from thinking straight too. When we got to the green room at the studios in Peterborough there was a woman in there I recognized, so I assumed she was someone in the industry I had met at one of the consumer shows. She looked quite glamorous and she was super-friendly, so I just got chatting away to her. Before long I realized she was another guest and was going on the hour before me – of course she was. Why else would she have been in there?

So I'm chatting away like we were long-lost friends, trying to calm my nerves, desperately hoping I didn't smell of vomit, and before long someone came to take her through to do the eight o'clock show. I was up next, on the nine o'clock show, and I was desperately trying to stay awake and alert. As she went out of the door, Simon looked at me with an expression of absolute bafflement and said, 'What are you doing? How on *earth* do you know her?' I was like, 'I don't know. We must have met before, when I was doing the screentest or something.'

'It's Linda bloody Lusardi,' he replied. 'You've never met her in your life.'

I gasped. I would never have chatted away to her like that if I'd known she was a celebrity, but she just seemed quite friendly! My distraction gone, that sick feeling returned to the pit of my stomach, where it had been for days now. I glumly wondered how Linda Lusardi's face creams were selling as I sat there as if I was waiting for my appointment at the gallows.

Then, just as 'my' hour began and I was starting to brace myself for my appearance, along came my old friend Pam Kershaw. She was hanging around that night as crafts were her thing and the Pick of the Day was some card-making kit she had booked. I thought it was terrible, though, and sales so far were not going well, which was making me feel ten times better about my slot.

So in swished Pam, not quite into the green room but peering in from the threshold. I could see Simon standing behind her as she looked at me in a slightly odd way.

'Hi, Sara,' she said, all cheery, as if she hadn't turned my life upside down a week ago. 'I'm just checking you're all right for your slot. And I'm wondering if, you know, well, if we have a real hit on our hands and it starts to sell . . . do you have any extras?'

And at first I was thinking, 'Is this the same woman I had a conversation with last week? Like, obviously she knows.'

'Well, yeah, I do,' I said quietly.

'Oh, excellent,' she replied. 'How many?'

The balance of how many you haven't ordered that I've made for you, pet. Obviously. Six and a half thousand, I thought.

Then I smiled and told her politely.

And she just laughed.

It was a moment I will never forget, and one that I hope I never have to relive.

It felt as if she was moments from saying, *Don't look at me like that, this is your own stupid fault*. And the truth of it is that it *was* my own stupid fault. I have never made that mistake again, and you can be sure I never will. You have to learn these lessons the hard way sometimes. And I don't mind telling you about this moment of absolute indignity ... in the hope you might learn from my mistake.

So let's say it again: don't *ever* manufacture anything without a purchase order. Even if somebody is saying it's the best product they've ever heard of and they're going to order thousands. Because that is very different from having a piece of paper that says, 'We are ordering thousands, and we'll be paying for them on this date.'

Even if you're a twenty-one-year-old and you're excited because it's your first-ever business order, remember the rule. Nothing without the purchase order.

Anyway, back to the show, which was about to go on air. It opened with a preview of all the products that were coming up, including mine. The Pick of the Day was that damn card-making kit, then the presenters casually said, '... and if you've got some extra glue and paper, we've got this new tool tonight which will help you make your own envelope to fit any size card that you've made ... but we'll be looking at that a little bit later.'

The first fifteen minutes of the show was spent on explaining the Pick of the Day, while my heart rattled away on the side of the set. But they must have seen a lot of pre-sales on the Enveloper as the programme started because the floor manager came over to speak to me.

'I know the show's written and we're planning to come to you at five to ten,' he explained, 'but actually, we're going to come to you early.'

'No problem,' I replied, thinking it might be two or three minutes earlier. But after only a few minutes I was on, the presenter asking me to explain the product live on air.

'Well, it does this and it does this, and this is how easy it is to do it,' I said to the camera, knowing that my finances were potentially on the line if I made a mess of things. The previous product's presenter had just demonstrated making a card with her kit, so I got them to bring the card over while I made the matching envelope for it so people could immediately make the connection.

The difference between the two products was that the card-making kit was a very specific one – it was all about fairies and fairy decorations and motifs. So, even if you're already into making cards, you have got to be quite seriously into fairies too. But, in theory, given that the hour was all about cards, every single person watching the show should want my product: because if you're into making cards, you have an immediate need for envelopes. My audience was hundreds of times bigger than hers was, I kept telling myself. It wasn't about fairies, or even design aesthetics. It was about functionality.

'Look, here's an envelope. Isn't that lovely? And easy!' I said with a flourish, as I showed my envelope next to the frilly fairy card.

The cameras went back to the Pick of the Day and that took centre stage once more. Only five minutes later the floor manager came over again.

'We're coming to you again, Sara. Another demonstration, if you would,' he whispered.

'But it's the same demonstration. I've already done it,' I said, starting to panic. I had only prepared a ten-minute demonstration, after being told my slot had been slashed. What was going on?

'Well, we're coming back for another demo in a couple of minutes, so can we do a different size or something?' came the reply, with a bit of a sense of urgency.

So the host – and the camera – comes back over to me and I gamely make another envelope – this time a slimline one. At this point I see Pam Kershaw tottering into the studio in her black patent shoes with a big black swirly dress floating around her as she wafts over to Simon, who I can see sitting at the back of the set watching my performance. Now I'm trying to fold bits of card, remember that I'm on TV and angle my head so I can see what's going on. A few minutes later I'm doing a third demo, but off-set in my eyeline Pam Kershaw leaves the room before wafting back in with a clipboard and a pen. Now Simon's signing something, and I still don't know what's going on. I do my next demonstration – a fourth! I'm just making all sorts of sizes now to keep the momentum going until the end of the hour, as I know we're into the last five minutes, which I knew would have been mine anyway.

At last the hour ended and I took a big exhale. At least now I would know how many we'd sold and how much I was going to owe Tony. From this point onwards, we could make a plan instead of being dependent on the whims of Pam Kershaw.

'What's going on?' I said to Simon as soon as I could. 'Why's Pam Kershaw been in to talk to you?'

'We've sold out,' he told me. Just matter-of-fact like that.

'Awww, brilliant, brilliant, we've sold out all fifteen

hundred! Can we manage to give her the other six and a half thousand?'

He was like, 'No, we've completely sold out.' And I was like, 'I *know*, so let's give her the six and a half thousand!'

'*No!* We've sold all eight thousand,' he said, exasperated with me. 'And they want to know if we can increase the order to fifteen thousand . . .'

'*Yes*, we can increase the order to fifteen thousand!' I replied. 'We'll go and get Tony to make the balance now!'

'They need it in forty-eight hours.'

I thought of my sister in her school uniform, wielding her hairdryer.

'Oh. No, we can't make seven thousand in forty-eight hours.'

Later that evening Simon was driving me home. I had been booked to appear on the next day's show too, but with no stock left to sell, we simply had to leave.

I didn't have to worry any more. We could cash Tony's cheque! But we now had to persuade him to get to work on making as many as he could. Before we knew it, he had put three lads on it, just churning them out. He doubled production, and we had to get some other people to start helping with the stickering because my poor sister couldn't cope with it all, alongside her homework.

From that day on, Tony would make them, and as soon as we had between four and five thousand, my dad would drive them in with my precious purchase order, book them into the warehouse, and within a few days I'd go down to Peterborough and do a show. And they kept selling out, so we just kept doing it. By Christmas, two months later, we had sold thirty thousand.

It was *the* product to have, the one that everybody was talking about that Christmas. And because I'd worked with Glenda and spent all that time selling into the shops, I knew which magazines to advertise in. I took a little £180 advertisement in the back of *Craft Business*, using my university flatmate as the hand model holding the product in the picture. I designed the ad myself on my clunky computer, sent it off to them from my flat and waited to see how the business would take off. Meanwhile, my university work was mounting up, which meant some serious burning of candles at both ends.

I used to study for the first couple of hours of the day, then from 9 a.m. to 5 p.m. I would work on the business: support calls, customer service calls, doing the mailings and, of course, all the admin. And there was only me, running what was very quickly a very successful business ... until five o'clock in the evening, when I would switch back to doing my studies.

Where I was living there were four other management students, so I trained them in a little bit of craft so that I could go out to lectures sometimes during the day, leaving them to answer the phone.

Back then, everything was done by fax, so I had a fax

machine installed in my university bedroom, as well as a laser printer. If a customer wanted to order an information pack, they would fax the request sheet through for one. Before long I was doing about fifteen a day. I would handwrite little notes to go in with the sheets I was printing off in my room, and head to the post office every day. The woman in the post office got to know me really well! And like the truly diligent sales-person I am, a couple of days later – between lectures – I would call each and every person who had asked for an information pack.

'Did you like the information pack?' 'Did you want to place an order?' 'I can take your details over the phone.'

These days – and even during last year's *Strictly* mayhem – if I ever look back and I feel like I'm really busy or that I've got a bit too much on, I just think back to that year. And I think, 'Yeah, this isn't that.' Because *that* was a crazy, crazy time in my life.

By January we had over two hundred shops stocking our little wooden Envelopers, and by the time I graduated the business was turning over half a million pounds. But I still graduated with a first-class honours degree that year as the highest-achieving student in the whole of the management school. Just as I had set out to do. When people always ask me 'What's your biggest achievement?', I think they always assume it's going to be getting my MBE, or TV work, but it isn't: it is that first-class honours degree.

Chapter 4

A Sprinkle of Magic

———

It all sounds fabulous, doesn't it? So high-powered, like we'd really made it. Well, let me tell you, we might have had the turnover, but we really hadn't made it. If anything, we were a serious case of faking it till we'd made it. There was no point in pretending I could carry on like this alone, even if I had finished my degree.

One evening my old schoolmate Meera called me and said, 'You know this little business you started? Well, you don't need any help, do you? Because I'm really worried about my mom . . .'

Meera comes from a very traditional Indian family, the Vijayaraghavans, the kind of family where her dad was a doctor and her mam had always been expected to stay at home and look after the family. But Meera was my age now, and she and her brother had gone – not just graduated but left home. And Meera knew how low her mom was getting at home with not much to do, so she said, 'Is there any chance she could come and work for you?'

'I don't really need anyone to work for me,' I explained. (Ignoring the obvious work mounting up around me but very aware that I couldn't really afford to pay any staff.)

'You don't have to pay!' said Meera (as though she had read my mind!). 'I just thought she could come and help you . . .'

'Well, I'm not having her help me and not paying her . . .' I said, indignant.

So we found a middle ground: I asked Kamala to come and work a couple of hours a day, because that is what the business could afford at that point. But, in reality, she often ended up staying way beyond those hours without ever asking for more wages. We developed something of a little system: I used to get the orders, and I would email them over to Kamala, who would come to my mam and dad's house, sit on the floor in our Helen's bedroom and download the details. She'd then go to Mam and Dad's shop round the corner, take payments on their PDQ machine, making sure to ring each customer to explain why their credit-card bill would say 'Wear Valley Decorating Centre' and not 'Crafter's Companion'. Then she'd pack the Envelopers in with a couple of bits of promo paper, take them to the post office, get them individually weighed and stamped up and send them off. And that's how we ran our whole dispatch area of the business.

Let me paint you a picture of how things were run back then, once I had graduated. From those very early days of the business, we had worked out of the same building that had been our family hub since before I was born. My dad had bought it as a derelict building and had slowly done it up. The wallpaper and paint shop had been run from the downstairs, with my dad's various other business ventures in a variety of outbuildings, cellars and garages.

At first the family lived on the premises, and then we built a bungalow on the grounds. I say 'grounds', but it was really a big garden with a bungalow twenty feet from the main building. So when I started Crafter's Companion and took on Kamala, we converted one of the little garages into an office and production space for the two of us.

At first, we *were* the whole team – customer services, accounts, the lot – even though we were pretending to be a staff of bigger than two. We had two cheapo phone handsets from Argos, and Kamala would answer the phone, 'Hello, Crafter's Companion. Can I help?' before saying, 'Yes, I'll just see if anyone in accounts/ customer services/production is available,' and putting her finger over the receiver, carrying the phone over to me on the other side of the room and mouthing which department I was meant to be before I started talking. The height of professionalism.

As for our marketing, I was blagging it there too. It was my opinion that if I advertised in print, instead of taking a quarter-page advert in four different magazines I should just take one full-page advert in one publication. Although fewer people would see it, it would look like we were a big deal to those who did.

But there was only so long this whole 'fake it till you make it' set-up could last. I eventually started saying, 'I think we should hire some more staff now,' but Kamala was dead set against it, convinced that us two working fourteen to sixteen hours a day was for the best, because she didn't trust anyone but us to care as much about the business.

When I finally persuaded her, it was only because I told her that there was a cracking lass I used to work with at Graphicus who had been a really smart admin person. I thought they would get on, that Sharon would fit in with us. She was on maternity leave at that point, so I convinced her not to go back to Graphicus … and the two of them are still with me fifteen years later. Sharon now manages all of our customer services globally, and Kamala has been a director for thirteen years.

It's been this style of recruiting that has always served

me best: not hiring someone for a certain skill but for being the right person. And we've developed their skills as they've made their way through the company. Kamala and Sharon are just the right calibre of people, who have developed their skill sets over the years and have gone on to prove themselves invaluable.

With Sharon's arrival, the team started to get a little bigger, so we just took over the next garage, and then the next. My parents had converted all of the first floor of the main building into residential flats by this point, eight of them, so when we got even bigger a few months later we put a staircase up to the first floor above the wallpaper and paint shop and turned that into offices too.

Every time we got bigger, we knocked through into the next flat, and we just kept going that way until the whole place was like a rabbit warren. We ended up taking the whole of that first floor. We just had people everywhere, and everyone was having to share desks. Then we had nowhere for staff to park, so we used to have to ask people to set up a lift share into work because we didn't have space for all the cars. It was so haphazard for so long because we were growing so fast.

We were still in those offices until we were turning over about £10 million a year and had about forty staff on site. And a big part of us reaching that size so fast was my star product, the one that really put me on the map in the industry – the Ultimate.

Our wooden Enveloper was going great guns in that

first year, but I had quickly had another idea: we could have that envelope-maker, and a board that folds cards, and the one that does boxes, and put them all together in one, adding a few bells and whistles and making it into the ultimate companion to any crafter. And that's literally what we called it!

I had the idea, drew it all out and worked with an industrial designer to get plans for making it. I was so excited. Then I went to get quotes for what it would cost to have made – and I was told it would be £100,000 to get the moulds made for the eighteen tools that would make up the Ultimate. Obviously, I didn't have £100,000 just sitting in the bank. And something I have always stuck to from day one with my business, and still stick with even to this day, is that if I don't have £100,000 in the bank, then we're waiting until I've got £100,000 before we spend £100,000.

I'd never borrowed money from someone else and used that to finance what we do in the business. It had always been self-financed growth, and the benefit of that is I never had to answer to anybody else. That feeling I had when I didn't know if I could pay Tony back for all those Envelopers is something I never want to experience again.

I didn't want to owe the bank any explanations, and I didn't want to owe anybody anything. But none of this grand thinking helped me to magic £100,000 into the bank.

So we went back to the drawing board. How could we get that cash fast enough? Then I realized that instead of using MDF for the Envelopers we could make the product in plastic (which only needed a £30,000 investment for that single tool), and that would reduce the unit cost, meaning I could make greater profit on each product. Sure enough, we made the switch, the sales came in, and after a few months we *did* have £100,000 in the bank. So I used that profit from my debut product to fund what became our flagship product. The Ultimate is what we became known for; it is my baby, my absolute pride and joy, and the product that took us international. We have sold a quarter of a million all over the world. But oh my god. What it took to get that first order out . . .

I had the idea in October 2006 and, once I'd had the prototype made, I went straight back to my friends at Ideal World. I showed them the product, did my full pitch, and they thought it was amazing. They did one big craft day a year and it was on 7 February. They were ready to put in an order. And this time, I made sure we had a purchase order number . . .

With the order *genuinely* confirmed, I asked the tooling company if we could make the stock that Ideal World wanted in time, and their reply was very simple: 'Not really, because it's October now and we haven't even started.' My reply was equally simple: 'Come on! We can do this! We can do it, I'm sure!'

This was very much my attitude all the time back then. I was twenty-three, remember.

So my enthusiasm persuaded them, and we agreed we *could* do it. They started making the tools straight away. But by December it was pretty damn obvious there was not a cat in hell's chance that we were going to manage to do what we'd promised. I went back to Ideal World and explained that we weren't on track to hit the 7 February deadline, but the guy there basically said, 'Well, you have to.'

'No, it's not possible. It really is not possible,' I explained. I was, as ever, confident that I could bend the situation to suit my will. But he was adamant.

'You've committed to it, so you have to meet the deadline.'

We tried so many times to get out of it, while still trying to do everything we could to make it. Needless to say, it got to 6 February, we were still committed to the show, and we'd still only made eight of the eighteen tools that we had to create to complete the number of products they wanted.

To do the show itself, I had to use semi-prototype tools, all held together with superglue, and with me totally fudging it. In the end, because they had to admit that we had given them lots of notice that we wouldn't make the date, Ideal World went on air with the line: 'We envisage this product is going to be so popular that we won't be able to dispatch them for three weeks.'

I don't know how I talked my way round that one, but my positivity forged the way, as ever. But I suppose it wasn't as if that line *wasn't* true – there *was* a lot of demand for the product: we literally sold the full ten thousand they'd ordered the first day I launched it! It was the biggest craft product they had ever sold, and immediately became one of their biggest-selling products ever. The place was buzzing and I was on an absolute high as Simon drove me home from Peterborough that night.

I had been too fraught with worry when I presented the Enveloper to think about much more than what I owed on the manufacture of the product, but the experience of launching the Ultimate was very instructive for me on the dynamics of shopping TV and how utterly reactive it is. It is one of the purest forms of live television, in that the producers and presenters are constantly – not just every hour but often up to the minute – responding to what the viewers at home are doing and whether they are spending or not. At the start of every show, each presenter has a target they are trying to hit, so if a guest is flopping, they yank them off and replace them with someone else, almost immediately. They are forever doing the TV equivalent of reading the room, a constant call-and-response going.

There are some 'celebrities' who go into TV shopping after an acting or modelling career, seeing it as something to do once their 'real' career is over, a bit of a retirement gig. They can treat it as a little bit below them, not wanting to admit that maybe it's the only work they are now getting.

But the people who become the real stars have usually come via another route: they've probably started as entrepreneurs and are used to having to sell their own product to a live audience. The dynamic on air is very similar to the dynamic on a market stall or a consumer show; they have the same mentality, the same thrill of the chase, the same reliance on being able to read – and fast – what the audience is thinking, whether they are making that emotional connection to what they're being told. Because it's the telling that is the key, not the selling. If you can nail the former, the latter will come.

As with market-stall selling, demonstrating at trade shows or even stand-up comedy, you have to be nimble with the story you're telling, confident and fast enough to change tack if you sense the mood in your audience isn't quite with you. When you're on a stall, at your stand in an expo centre or on stage in a live venue, you can see those first flickers of people losing interest and you have to have the steeliness (and the sense of fun!) to whip something else out from under your sleeve. I hadn't had a market stall, but I'd long since seen my dad on one, and I'd had those crucial months running the stall for Graphicus at those consumer shows all over the country, knowing that I had to make a certain number of sales in order to save the company.

The only difference with live television is that it's the producer who has to tell you what the audience is doing rather than you reading it yourself. Your ability to respond in seconds has to be the same, though.

The thing to remember about the TV shopping channels is that they have always got buyers out at trade shows, on the lookout for the latest and greatest thing. But it's not necessarily the products they are always looking at ... it's the presenters. When you walk around a trade show, it's always the stands with the demonstrations that catch your eye, isn't it? You want to be part of that magic moment, the big reveal, when they show how *their* product will change your life, how much happier you'll be with it, how wonderful it is that you've had this chance to find out about it.

So, as the buyers make their slow, discreet prowl up and down the aisles of the trade shows, they're keeping an eye out for products, yes. And they're looking for demonstrators, yes. But what they are really, really hoping to find is a storyteller. *They* are the sprinkle of magic.

Years later, when I joined QVC in America, I distinctly remember them explaining to me that their number-one choice to have on representing a brand is the company founder or the person who invented the product. Because *that* person can actually say that they saw the problem and decided to solve it. *They* have the story, and they can tell the story like nobody else can.

Their second choice would be to have someone from the company who maybe isn't the inventor or founder but works for the company full time and has totally bought into that product. And then the third choice, which a lot of companies do, is to have a professional whose job is to sell products on the TV shopping channels – and they are very good at it. But they're more like actors, and they represent several brands.

If you were setting up a company and didn't have the trade-show experience, you would probably assume that the best thing for television would be to hire somebody who's at the top of their game, who's selling stuff all the time. But for the TV shopping channels, that would be their third choice, because there's no authenticity there. The presenter is acting out the story. They might be doing it well – really well – but they'll always be acting.

And I think the channels are right – they've had nearly fifty years of experience, and it remains true that people want the story, the experience, as much as the product. When you watch the shows, you can see when people really feel it, which is why I continue to go on television all over the world to sell our products. I'll fly out to Germany and do presentations on a German shopping channel, despite the fact that I don't speak a word of German and they are paying through the nose for a lady to live lip-synch me: because my passion and enthusiasm and body language ooze out of my every pore. It's *my* company, it was *my* family home we took over with Enveloper sawdust, and it's *my* family who continues to work there. And customers are well within their rights to enjoy that connection – I know I do!

When I was doing this presentation for the Ultimate, I was still going by instinct, but I have since been through so many professional training courses and I've learned that only 7 per cent of what we communicate is through the actual words we say. The other 93 per cent is all made up of your intonation, your body language, how you know to get that across.

I didn't know it then, but that night, as I unveiled the product that was going to make me, I was the TV-shopping-channel dream, because I had invented the product and I wanted to share that information with the viewers. I was proud to – I was bursting to!

It is this passion that continues to run through Crafter's Companion: each time I'm on air presenting a new range or a seasonal product, I have either invented or been heavily involved in the development of that product. I've got that passion for it that nobody can replicate, which is why as well as doing most of my own presenting I also always choose people who are crafters themselves to work on TV within my company.

Basically, to end up working on TV for me, you can guarantee that I've spotted you as a customer and thought you had a talent and then trained you, or I've seen you working in one of our shops. You had to have been enjoying it – feeling that paper under your finger-tips and enjoying folding it yourself – before you can start doing it professionally. Because you really can't fake the passion to get on the payroll. There are only ten people in the whole company who do this, and every single one of them has followed this route. Show-manship is real, but passion is even more real.

I have seen companies, especially within the craft industry, who are selling products that you really do not need. They are useless, bad quality, whatever. How-ever, they have got such a compelling storyteller behind the company and in front of the camera that the busi-ness can perform really, really well on TV. Because the people watching just buy into the mood.

This means that when I'm on television I'm selling myself first and foremost. I'm endearing myself to that audience. I'm getting them to trust me, so that when I say to them, 'This crummy envelope situation is a genuine problem you are facing in your life, you know – your cards aren't good enough until they've got a matching envelope,' they trust me. And when I tell you straight afterwards that I have a solution, they are delighted.

For example, I *could* explain that if you go to a high-street shop like Hobbycraft to buy some envelopes for some cards you might have made, you might walk down the envelope aisle and see a pack of envelopes that are the right size-ish for £3.99, but I have invented a tool which makes all sorts of envelopes for just £9.99. And the customer would probably look at the two of them and think, 'I'm going to buy the pack of envelopes because that looks like too much hard work over there. Plus, it looks really complicated. I've no idea how to do it, but I know where I am with a plain pack of envelopes.'

But if you're watching Ideal World on a Tuesday night at nine o'clock and you see this girl on there making some cards and you watch me having the absolute time of my life, looking like I could not be more excited, saying to you, 'I can't believe you've just spent hours making that beautiful card. And then you're gonna spoil the effect it makes by putting it in a plain white envelope that's probably the wrong size. You wouldn't wrap a fantastic present up in a bit of old newspaper, would you? Oh *no*, you would wrap it in beautiful wrapping paper and put a gorgeous bow on it. And that's what we're doing here: we've got a card, and we're finishing it off in a gorgeous handmade envelope, made in the matching fancy paper that costs pennies, and it only takes seconds. Basically, you're gonna have this tool for the rest of your life, and it's going to cost you a fraction of a penny each time you use it. Realistically, over the years you have this tool, your card-giving experience is never going to be the same – it's going to be elevated.'

And by the time you finish listening to me, you are

convincing yourself that a) you need to go and make cards pronto if you don't already and b) when you do, you never want to put them in a plain white envelope again, you're always going for a matching envelope, and c) oh my god, isn't that girl having the best time of her life? If I spend £9.99 today, I'm hoping to be as happy as she is.

What I've done is I've sold you the dream. I've painted a picture of a problem that you probably didn't even know you were having. And then I've given you a solution to it that seems like such a no-brainer that the only thing you can think of to do is pick up the phone and order that item. And that's how TV shopping works.

The more hours you do on air, the more confident you become. There is nothing more exhilarating than standing there, on air, and somebody is pumping into your ear, 'We've got X number of people on the phone lines! X number of people on the website ordering! This is becoming a smash hit – you've sold 60 per cent of your stock! Come on! Go for it! We're ahead of our target!' Nothing beats that buzz. (Or at least I thought nothing did, until last autumn, when I discovered dancing the cha-cha-cha in front of a live TV audience.)

But back then, when *Strictly* was still a dream, Simon drove me home from Peterborough and I was glowing with the success of my slot on air. My product was going to be a success! I had done it! Then, the truth slowly dawned that we'd told all the customers that they would be receiving their product in three weeks, and the order was far from complete. The first thing I did was go to see my dad and look at the production schedules. We worked out where we were and, in short, we were pretty screwed. We still hadn't tooled the ruler that went in the middle or the little hinges, and quite a lot else. But we *had* done the big outer boards.

The little joinery company in our village had not been making the Envelopers since we moved from MDF to plastic – they were now being done by a manufacturing plant in nearby Hexham, way out in the Northumberland countryside, which my Business Link mentor Richard Hall had helped me to source. But they had no way of being able to cope with an order this big for the Ultimate. They were just eight staff who worked nine to five, and when we ran through the calculations we realized that even if the place ran twenty-four hours a day, seven days a week, we still couldn't get to ten thousand in three weeks. But my dad and I were absolutely determined to get this order done, so we put our heads together and tried to find a way round it.

We came up with a two-pronged attack. First of all, we found a bigger manufacturing plant over in Aycliffe that was willing to take on a couple of the tools which made up the Ultimate. And then my dad paid a visit to Hexham, determined to persuade them to help us.

As you now know, my dad can persuade almost

anyone to do anything, so after the guys up in Hexham had had a meeting with us – where he gave them one of his very best 'We will find a way!' talks – they were convinced that the best course of action was basically to hand over the keys to their factory to us.

Richard, the chap who ran it, really must have trusted my dad, because the faith he placed in us was remarkable. That factory was his pride and joy – he collected koi carp, so he had this eight-foot-deep pond that he'd built in the reception area. He was so proud of it. You came into this lovely fancy reception with these koi carp, and then you went through this little door, and he had about eight machines in there. And tool-makers as well. He could do everything, from designing the product to making the tool: 'the tool' is basically like the mould; you make it out of steel, and then the tool goes into position in one of the machines and you shoot the plastic into it to make the plastic product itself.

So this tiny team of Richard's agreed that they would staff the workshop until ten o'clock every night, and after that we had to staff it until the morning. And when I say 'we', I think that what we had was me, my mam, Kamala, Sharon, and an absolute assortment of various friends and family who I could persuade to help out.

What we ended up doing was having one of my dad's friends drive to Aycliffe every morning to pick up all the pieces they'd worked on overnight, then he'd drive to Hexham, drop them off, pick up whatever we'd managed to make and complete, drive that load to Peterborough, drop it off, come back to sleep for so many hours and then do it all again the next day. Anybody I could find to help, any pairs of hands that were prepared to come along every night at ten o'clock to Hexham, I'd have. We'd get there and there'd be all sorts – one night there was this woman I'd never met. I was like, 'Hi. Nice to meet you, I'm Sara.' And she's like, 'Hey, I'm your Aunty Ann,' and it turns out it was Simon's aunty! Anybody could come, anybody who could make it – my little cousins, even my Aunty Lynn after finishing a shift at fire-brigade control – so that we'd have between ten and fifteen staff every night to keep the machines going.

We would have to work the assembly lines all night. And I'm saying all this, but it's probably highly, highly illegal. We had no health and safety. My dad was the bloody foreman who was running the place, we had people like my mam, who had been working in the family shop all day and then would work through the night every night, gluing the feet on to the Ultimates. We just did anything we could to make it happen. Little Kamala (she is literally little – she's five foot two) was operating two 270-ton Battenfeld machines, which are, like, twice the size of a table, the kind of thing you see in a geography video at school about 'manufacturing plants'. This was a factory that was making car parts all day as a crucial part of the North-East's motor industry, and now it was on mauve Ultimates by night!

The Battenfelds were needed to run the big outer parts for the Ultimate, but these ones were a good thirty or forty years old. They had two of these machines that were side to side, and every sixty-five seconds it would start a new cycle. The two sides would shoot together, and then you'd hear the plastic being squirted in. It would show you on the little computer screen next to it how many seconds of plastic injection you had left. Then there was twenty-five seconds of cooling time, before a loud beep, and then you'd slide the glass door back, the pump valve would pull backwards and it would push the part off. Then you'd have to lean in, grab the parts, close the door, press the button and the process would start again. Then, with the finished board, there would be a little piece of excess plastic coming out – the 'sprue'. We'd have to take a little Stanley knife and cut it off, nice and clean, for a smooth edge, so you couldn't see the point where the plastic had been injected in.

Basically, you had sixty-five seconds between cycle times, but there were two machines back to back, so you had about thirty seconds to cut the sprue off, stick on the feet then put the finished part on the pile. Then you'd have to turn around to the other machine, slide the door open, and so on. It was proper physical work, so when I'd see little Kamala on her tiptoes operating these two massive 270-ton Battenfeld machines at four o'clock in the morning, I felt overwhelmed with gratitude. We all had to take it in turns, because more than an hour on those Battenfelds and you'd be knackered. We had to spread out a few people on the assembly lines: someone on the little machine that's putting out the ruler, one on the little cutting tool, one on the hinge machine, which popped off eight hinges every twenty-five seconds.

This went on for hour after hour after hour. There were always empty pizza boxes everywhere, as food was how I got everyone through the night. One morning at about 3 a.m. I found my mam sitting in the corner, rocking backwards and forwards, just crying. And I went over and I said, 'Mam, what's the matter? What on earth's happened?'

'My fingers are stuck together,' she told me, holding up her hand to show me. She was just so tired, there was so much emotion flying around. And quite a lot of glue.

We did manage to unstick my mam's fingers, but I look back and think what my family, Simon's family, our friends – everybody – achieved for us by rallying around in those three weeks. It was absolutely off the chart. These days, I love telling new staff at Crafter's Companion this story. The look on their faces when they hear, awe-struck, what we did – and probably should not have done! I want them to know that we rolled up our sleeves and got stuck in in the early days, and I get a lot back as a result.

It was risky. It was probably breaking the law in terms of employment practice. It's astounding to think that we took control of a factory and filled it with staff who weren't qualified, with no health and safety regulations or anything, operating every night for twenty-two nights . . .

And we didn't do it. We had twenty-one days, and we did it in twenty-three. When we had finally delivered the last two hundred, the foreman at Ideal World rang my dad and said to him, 'How does it feel, Frank, to have been so close but to have failed at the eleventh hour?' And after what we'd been through for those three weeks, my dad never forgave him. There was no penalty for the late delivery, but they sure enjoyed rubbing our noses in it.

But still to this day, the Ultimate is the only product ever in the history of the craft industry to win a major innovation award in the UK, the US and Europe the year it was launched – something I am immensely proud of!

Almost more importantly, though, that experience gave me an insight into that world, something not many others had at that stage in the growth of their company. Very few business owners have stayed up all night to engage in the sweat and graft of physically making their own product. I would imagine that not many twenty-three-year-old women have an understanding of the manufacturing process that ran as deep as mine did by then – and my knowledge has only grown because of that solid early experience.

Quite a few of my *Dragons' Den* investments have been products like this. It's one thing to have worked in a company that designs and manufactures products, but it doesn't mean you've ever been into the factory and physically made them yourself. So now, whenever I'm negotiating with a firm – we still do a lot of it here in the UK, and with some in China – I like to invest in the firm itself too. These days I am part owner of the plastic moulding company ten minutes down the road that works on a huge number of our products.

Say a much bigger company has fifteen machines, the updated version of the Battenfelds we were using then. All the machines are being used on great, well-earning jobs, and I come along and want a batch of Ultimates making. They're not going to suddenly take a job out of the machine that's producing however many pounds an hour profit to run my little thing. Of course they're not! Whereas if I spend £100,000 of my own, buy a Battenfeld machine and put it in their factory, I can say, 'Right, whenever I want an Ultimate, make them in my machine. And when my machine's not making my Ultimates, I'm gonna rent it back to you. You can borrow it off me and use it at a fraction of the cost you pay on your other machines, which are all on hire purchase.' It's a way of guaranteeing my own production without having to actually open my own factory – genius!

It just makes complete business sense, and gives me the control to say, 'Drop everything. Put my tool in and make Ultimates this afternoon.' They have to, because it's my machine. But I only really understood that because I had been part of a rag-tag bunch of friends and family letting ourselves in past the koi carp and on to the factory floor, night after night. An experience none of us have ever forgotten.

Chapter 5

TV Shopping till You're Dropping

There's one small thing that I forgot to mention about the period when we were growing the business and creating the Ultimate, which is that I was trying to break the United States at the same time. From day one of Crafter's Companion, I was very much of the opinion that whatever we were doing in the UK, America was the land of opportunity. However many crafters there are here in the UK, there were likely to be ten times more over there. So I started the company on 24 October 2005, and by the following January I was on a plane out to America, ready to crack the US market, determined to sell Envelopers everywhere, to everyone.

As a first step, I decided to take myself off to Las Vegas to the big trade show of the year, CHA (Craft and Hobby Association). Bearing in mind what I told you a few chapters ago about how I couldn't even face going down to London to do my placement year from university, you can imagine how I felt about heading to Nevada. It wasn't just because I didn't want to not be with Simon, but because I really am a proper country bumpkin. Even today I live five minutes from where I grew up, and I have tried at every stage to keep as much of my business there as possible. I used to get the heebie-jeebies just getting on a train to London, and now I reckoned I was just going to turn up in Las Vegas on my own for a ten-day business trip?

I look back now and I kind of can't believe my mam and dad even let me go. I had done it the cheapest possible way, so I was getting the train down to London, staying overnight at a mate's parents' house, and then my mate was taking me to Gatwick Airport the next day, because that's where the cheapest flights to Las Vegas flew from. Given that I had started crying at Darlington train station, it really was a long journey.

I was absolutely dreading being away on my own, doing all that international travel with no one at all for company, so the minute I came across some other people from the craft industry at the airport, I latched on to them like a bloody leech. There was a group of about five or six of them, all from the same company, which was exhibiting at CHA. I had seen them around at trade shows in the UK before and worked out who they were, and I was so relieved to see them I couldn't stop talking to them, even offering to be an extra pair of hands setting up their stand just so I wouldn't be on my own! My plan for that whole trip was just to turn up with a suitcase full of the original wooden Envelopers, walk around and talk to as many people as possible and see what I could make of it.

Despite my nerves about being away from home, I was desperate to soak up as much as I could, to learn everything about how the industry worked in the US, to study the market and the big names, and to work and enhance my contacts wherever possible. When I think about it now, I can't believe that was me – being so confident about putting myself forward – but I think I was just driven by a desperation to get the company established. I didn't feel I could breathe out yet, there was so much to achieve.

'Sure, sure, I'll be by in the morning,' I said as we waited in baggage control. All I really wanted was an excuse to keep talking to them. 'Just let me know what hotel you're staying at.'

'The Mirage,' came the answer. *Bloody hell, that must be costing an arm and a leg*, I thought. It was one of the really fancy ones on The Strip!

I cleared customs, found a taxi and was driven to my hotel, which I had found online and paid pennies for. The first thing I noticed was that it was a long way from The Strip. Like, a *long* way from The Strip. The second thing I noticed was that the people outside seemed, maybe, kind of sleazy? Then, as we pulled up outside, I was thinking, '*What* have I done?'

I got my case out, walked into the hotel lobby, took a look around and thought, 'I'll not make it through the week alive.' It wasn't just that there were call girls everywhere, and pictures of call girls everywhere, it was more that their customers were everywhere. So I turned on my heel, hoping the cab was still there, and got straight back into the rear seat, saying, 'Take me to The Mirage.'

I am the tightest person ever. Ever. If you ask my friends about me, that will be one of the first things they'll tell you! But on that occasion, which was the first where I had ever felt truly vulnerable, a woman alone in a huge city with very little experience, it really felt like life or death.

As the cab pulled up to The Mirage I realized what a huge, grand hotel this really was, and all I could think was 'Woah, how much is this gonna cost?', but I had some decent Enveloper cash in the bank already, so I just walked up to the desk, handed over my company credit card and said, 'I need a room for nine nights, please.'

It was more per night than my whole stay would have been at the other hotel. And it was the fanciest hotel I'd ever been in in my life. So as I handed over that card I knew that I had to make that trip count. Not just pay for itself, but really, truly count. So I was up at six the next morning, loitering in reception for about an hour, waiting to bump into the contacts I had met at the airport.

When they appeared, I tried to look dead casual, all 'Oh, you guys mentioned you were here and, you know what, I thought it would be a nice treat, seeing as I'm travelling without the rest of my team ... Did you say you needed some help setting up?' And that was it.

For the rest of the week, I was up at the same time every day. I went to every breakfast seminar going, and I listened to every person in the industry who was giving a talk, and at the end of every one of those talks I would go and introduce myself.

'I'm Sara, I've got this product that makes envelopes. Do you think anybody would be interested? Who should I speak to?' I literally talked to anybody and everybody who would listen to me.

I walked the trade show itself several times, introducing myself to every stand-holder, piecing together the market, figuring out the key players, educating myself about what the barriers to doing business over there might be. Every day I woke up and thought, 'What can I learn?' And every evening I would just try and latch on to people that I'd met during the day, throwing in, 'What are you doing tonight? Oh yeah, I'm going to the same place – I'll see you there.' The energy of youth? The confidence of youth? Or just the desire to make nine nights at The Mirage worth it? A little bit of each, I imagine . . .

There was a UK pavilion of sixteen other companies that were exhibiting, and I spent a lot of time in there, learning what they had done in their early days, why they had done it that way, and what they were doing now. It was an enormous fact-finding mission, and even though I was missing home with every fibre of my body – even from the luxury of the hotel – it remains true even to this day that that trip was absolutely crucial to my success in the US.

Not doing a trip like this is where a lot of companies go wrong. I knew I wanted to go out in January with a view to being ready to exhibit the following year. All it cost me was the hotel and my flight. Whereas a lot of other companies head off to the land of opportunity and take a stand at a huge exhibition or trade show the very first time. They're immediately spending tens of thousands of pounds, and they still don't know anything about the market. So they arrive with the expectation of writing a multimillion-dollar order, and that is the only thing they judge the success of the show on. But they haven't done the prep work, they haven't got ready for the show in any real sense, so of course many of them come home with their head in their hands.

There was one company out of the sixteen in the UK contingent that had approached the market the way that I was doing: they had gone to the show several years in a row, and that year was the first year they were exhibiting and spending money. They knew the market, they had lined up distributors, they'd already worked out how they were going to ship their product, and only now were they advertising it. The other fifteen companies were turning up with a blank order book and simply hoping to write loads of orders in it. Of course, most of them headed back to the airport having spent tens of thousands on a show with no return, whereas the company that had actually put in work over the years came away having had a great show.

So I kept my eye on the company's owner over the week – Leandra Franich was her name. I watched what she did, learned from that and modelled myself on it for the next trip. And I think that's a key differentiator between how I've succeeded in business over in America as against a lot of other companies who have failed. Because it might be the same products that we sell in the US and the UK. But the way the market is structured, the way the distribution channels work, the way the customers behave, are all entirely different. And you need to learn that.

It's like those signs you see when you arrive at international airports that say that doing business in different territories is different every time – they're right! The naive companies are the ones that just assume it's the same everywhere. 'I'm successful in the UK. So I'm just going to pick up and do exactly the same in America and I'll be successful there.' But that's arrogance! It will never work!

In my opinion, that knowledge of *how little I knew* was essential. When I was in the UK, there was almost no situation I had encountered where I couldn't either draw a parallel to how I had seen my parents working as I'd grown up or talk to my parents for advice or inspiration. But my dad had never done any business outside of our county, let alone our country, so he had – and he knew he had – absolutely nothing to offer me in terms of support for our global business. And a skill I think I was lucky to be born with but have worked hard to develop further is that I can recognize what I'm not good at. I'm not frightened to say that. I understood and appreciated that I didn't know a thing about international business and that there was no shame in that. How could I have done? I was barely in my twenties!

So, prior to this trip, I took myself on a couple of courses, keen to learn as much as I could. And I tried to find mentors – which is something I still do today. Mentors come in two different types: mentors who know they're mentoring you, and mentors who have no idea you exist. The first are people you meet along the way, people you actively ask for advice. And the second are people you look up to, who you might follow on LinkedIn or whose autobiographies you might read, or whose interviews you might watch. They are mentoring you, just without talking back to you. And because of this, I have had hundreds of mentors, people who would never in a million years even know they had mentored me. And it was armed with many of these people's advice that I approached the American market.

As a result, one of the main things I learned at this show was that while card-making was big business over in the UK (and everybody interested in making cards therefore needed envelopes), it was different in the US – card-making hadn't really taken off in the same way. They all did the scrapbooking thing instead so, consequently, nobody was that interested in my Enveloper. I'm pleased to be able to let you know, though, that it turned out we were just a little bit ahead of our time. But my god am I glad I figured it out before I had spent any serious cash!

I went back to the States that summer and learned more, then the following year I headed to the same trade show, and this time I took a stand. It was only a little while after this that the buyer from HSN, the Home Shopping Network, approached me.

It sounds grand and glitzy, doesn't it? 'She was discovered at twenty-two in Las Vegas …' But, as ever, the truth was a little less glamorous. For starters, I only had a tiny little stand and, as is my way, I had done it in the cheapest way I possibly could in order not to need to borrow any money from anyone else.

This time I was staying at a cheaper – although not actively dangerous – hotel. I had printed my own pamphlets up. I had my laptop, and I had even taken a computer monitor over with me so that I could put my little videos on the screen. But I wasn't prepared to pay thousands of dollars to ship goods over there – I literally loaded everything into my own suitcases and carried it over with me. The home-printed pamphlets, the computer monitor, even the giant wooden replica Enveloper my dad had made me, which was in four pieces, and which I had to screw together and paint as part of setting up my stand. But it felt like my lucky mascot: a supersized Enveloper to try and catch everyone's attention.

I just paid excess baggage when I arrived. When you do a trade show in America, it's all run by the unions, which means that you have to send your shipping via them and the whole thing costs a fortune unless you're an enormous company. It's so complicated. So I figured it was so much easier just to have everything in suitcases and lug it about myself.

Simon had taken a week off work, but he couldn't take too much time, so I had to fly out on my own, with him following on a couple of days later. And the US show was on at the same time as another one I had decided was essential – in Frankfurt. So my mam and dad came to Frankfurt with me, we did the show there and I left my mam and dad to do the last day and to pack up while I flew straight from Frankfurt to Anaheim, where the US show was that year.

I built my replica Enveloper and put my little monitor screen up and started the show. I had toughened up a fair bit by now. I was more used to audiences abroad, I had more experience on television in the UK, and of course I had learned my trade at all those shows doing the demos of the Graphicus products. I was also more aware than ever of what the scouts for the TV networks were after and tried to lean into that.

I have a big personality, and I knew I could keep a crowd going around me if I started a demonstration. So before long, buyers who were on the hunt for demonstrable products – and storytellers – started to walk by and take a look. At first they'd just watch, then the next day a buyer, whose name I instantly recognized as being absolutely key in the industry, told me that I had a great story and a highly demonstrable product, which ticked all the boxes for her channel.

This woman was only an assistant buyer at the time, but I knew the influence she had. When she came over on the first day she said, 'This is my business card. I'm from HSN shopping channel. Have you heard of us?' And I said, 'Yes, I have, and in all honesty, I came out here in the hope that you would walk on to my stand: my products are designed to be sold on TV.

That's where I've had success in the UK, so my whole aspiration with this show was to hook up with you guys or any other TV shopping channels around the world.'

She smiled, and I realized that this was it. If I have ever had a 'this is my moment' moment, it was then.

'This is a dream come true for me,' I said. 'I just want to know how we can make this work because, look, I'm a proven success on the UK shopping channel. Let me show you the clips of my show, let me talk to you about how it's working and how I can replicate that with you guys over in America.'

She said she wanted me on the channel! But she also said that she had a problem. Because I had this tiny little stand, was so clearly doing everything on an absolute shoestring, *and* I was from the UK, she knew that the first thing her bosses would ask her was: 'Well, is her company actually of the magnitude that it can *cope* with many thousands of dollars' worth of orders? Can she finance it? Can she afford to do it? Can she afford the risk?'

And she was right to worry – doing a deal like this with a small, inexperienced company could have put it at huge risk of overtrading. That is the term for when a business grows at an unexpectedly fast rate. You suddenly require new staff, new stock, new ways to manufacture your stock and maybe even resources like warehousing and distribution, which all massively increase costs. You might – as I had learned in the past – put yourself in a position of being unable to deliver on your contracts and then not being able to pay for the new resources you have had to bring in. The whole thing can collapse if you're not careful, and I was glad that someone interested in me was also bearing these things in mind.

She came back to see me on the second day, and by the time she came back on the third day she'd spoken to her bosses and worked out what the time frame could be, how we could work it so that we could actually, physically, have a serious conversation about me working with them.

To this day, Marissa Larson, the same woman who spotted me then, is still our account manager. She has been promoted and promoted at the network and is now very senior there. But we are now very good friends and even better colleagues. She was just absolutely brilliant from day one. A lot of buyers can be snooty, knowing that they can make or break brands. Whereas Marissa just genuinely cared about me and the company, to the point whereby I know that when she had to present my product and my business to get approved, she really went above and beyond for us.

Once I had gone back to the UK, I'd made loads of samples of cards and boxes and envelopes and sent them out to her for her big pitch. But they got damaged in the post on the way, so she watched my DVD the night before, looked at all the damaged samples and sat up late at home, re-creating everything I'd made so that she could present it to her boss as successfully as possible. How many buyers would ever do that? Not many, I can tell you. She was so invested in me succeeding that to this day I feel like it's a partnership. Usually with these big companies it's just give and take: we give, they take take take. But I have had an amazing relationship with our buyer. She genuinely cares about me, and that's what made me feel very positive about the whole experience. She's always treated me with the same respect, back when I was a tiny little fish, and now that I'm the biggest fish in the craft pond. And it goes to show that you can be friends with people in business as well as having a great business relationship.

The first time I ever appeared on the Home Shopping Network, however, was one of the most exhausting, terrifying, yet thrilling days of my life. Largely because, fuelled by self-confidence and our relative UK success, I had not appreciated how different appearing on television in the land of opportunity would be. The networks in the UK were very, very tiny ponds compared to the US ones, which were the ocean. After all, they had invented the concept of TV shopping.

The UK channels – well, there is no denying that they are the lower-budget end of television. And as far as my broadcast experience went, Ideal World was the only studio I had ever been to, at home or otherwise. I had never set a foot in any BBC studio or anything like that at this point. But because I was broadcasting regularly over in the UK, Marissa had arranged that I wouldn't have to fly to the US for a screen test, as most of the other would-be presenters did. Instead, I could just send over a copy of a tape of my work for Ideal World and get approval on that.

It worked – they did approve the tape, although they also sent back some notes strongly suggesting that I take some elocution lessons to help with the fact that my strong North-East accent was causing some confusion. They were saying I spoke too fast, and I needed to remedy that before I could go on air. So I booked one elocution lesson, and I went and sat down in front of the coach and declared that I refused to lose my accent because I'm proud of where I'm from. I did ask for some help slowing things down, though.

They duly gave me some exercises, but they were expensive, those lessons, and I really couldn't help thinking that I already knew how to talk a bit more slowly. I mean, you just slow down. There was no point me going every week and just practising and speaking slowly, I thought. I could practise on my own, couldn't I? Basically, I just thought, 'Yeah, I've got this,' and never went back.

The day that HSN wanted me to make my debut on the channel was only hours after I was booked to do a big show on Ideal World in the UK, so I tried to use the time difference between the continents to my advantage and do them both. It seemed like a perfect plan: I would do the launch of a Pick of the Day at nine o'clock at night in Peterborough, and again at midnight, finishing at three o'clock in the morning. Simon was then going to drive me from Peterborough to Manchester airport, where we'd get the eight o'clock flight heading for Orlando, Florida, that morning. We'd land at three o'clock in the afternoon, and Simon would drive me to Tampa, where the studios are. I was scheduled to arrive at six o'clock the following night. Then I would have time to take a look around the studios and get my bearings, before going live at midnight.

What I hadn't really taken on board was that the first time I would ever set foot in a US TV studio, I wouldn't have slept for thirty-six hours. And they are absolutely enormous. Not just enormous, but with an apparently infinite number of actual studios. There were just the two on Ideal World, but here they were labelled Studio A, Studio B, Studio C, and so on, all the way up to G or H. And each of their studios is three or four times the size of one at Ideal World. And then – and this was the kicker – there are no camerapeople in any of them. None at all. Just the seven robotically operated cameras, all focused on you. On TV shopping channels in the UK, you have three cameras and three camerapeople operating what look like twenty-year-old cameras. Here – nothing. It looks like something out of the space age, or at least the key scene from that Jennifer Lawrence movie *Joy*.

The worst of it was that, as they showed me around, it was becoming quickly apparent that the TV execs there were clearly assuming that I was completely *au fait* with all of this, and I was just having to go along with it. At one point someone came up to me and said, 'Here you go, I've got your IFB for you.' Well, I didn't even know what an IFB was, and my brain certainly wasn't working fast enough to say, 'What the hell is an IFB?' The next thing I knew, some woman was sticking this IFB, which turned out to be an earpiece, in my ear and, all of a sudden, I've got voices in my head.

Well, I'd never, ever had voices in my head in my life. I know now what it's like, because I have it all the time, and I even know that IFB stands for interruptible foldback, and it's how everyone presenting live television – from the news headlines to the football to *Strictly Come Dancing* – can hear the gallery, which is where the producer, the director, the floor guys, the sound guys are all liaising with you. Fair enough, it's a great system, but until that morning I had never, ever experienced it. And I was too embarrassed to admit it. 'I can't cope with this. I don't know what to do,' I thought. And they just thought I was better than I was because they'd seen this tape of me on TV in the UK and assumed it was the same sort of channel they ran.

The next thing was Make-up, which I'd never experienced before either, because the shopping channels over here just don't have any budget for that. I had barely sat in the chair when they started to spray on the foundation. Literally spray it on from a sort of canister. And it was orange. They were absolutely caking me in make-up at the same time as backcombing my hair; it was getting higher and higher, absolutely massive. I'm looking at myself in the mirror, and I knew I was really tired, but honestly, I didn't even recognize myself. It was amazing, the total commitment to the glamour and just the overwhelming sense of it all being EXTRA. But really scary at the same time. I just had this little white top on, because I thought it was smart. It was half orange by the time I got on air. I had no fashion sense at all. I really did not know what I was doing, on very many levels.

But what I did know was how savage the system is over there. You are only ever as good as your last show. People are disposable unless they are shifting product. So I knew that I had to nail this appearance, and that it was my one and only opportunity. I was so aware that TV shopping was the key to my being successful in the US market. If I didn't get it right, there was no coming back, and I knew it. It was an enormous amount of pressure, especially as I had physically shipped hundreds of thousands of pounds' worth of Envelopers, which were now in their warehouses ready to go. If my appearance wasn't a hit, I would be having all of them delivered back to my warehouse, pronto.

The main thing was, I knew I had to speak slowly. Just keep things nice and slow. I was so tired I felt as if I was slowing down a bit anyway, but I was determined not to scramble my words in the excitement of it all. The trouble was, I had planned to be on air for an hour. By now, I was a big enough presenter on Ideal World that they regularly gave me an hour. They knew I could fill it comfortably, they knew I could sell enough stock to make it worth everybody's while, and they knew it was a system that worked. And because it was a tape of this that HSN had been sent, I had somewhere along the way picked up the idea that this was what they had booked me for. As such, I had a suite of products with me, not just the Enveloper: I had developed a card- and box-maker to go with it, to really push the idea of card-making in the US, where they were still more keen on scrapbooking.

Swept up in the excitement of it all, and confident in my abilities in a familiar studio, I had completely for-gotten to confirm this key piece of information: my timings. And now someone was leading me towards the studio and talking about how I had six or seven minutes. How was I supposed to sell the 93 million homes that I was broadcasting to the beauty of my

Enveloper in only seven minutes when I had prepared a demonstration that lasted an hour – *and* do it without talking quickly?

But there wasn't time to wallow in the catastrophe, I just had to get on and do it. So there I was, in the studio, with these unfamiliar voices in my head telling me which camera to look at and when, and trying to take it slowly – but also quickly.

After four minutes, I could tell that I was a total flop. Most of their roster of presenters were established; they didn't have to sell themselves or their craft to the audience – they knew they had tuned in because they were already interested. But here I was having to sell myself *and* sell the customers on the idea of wanting to make cards … *and* sell them on the product itself. Without going too fast!

I could practically hear the other presenters in the sidelines with their products licking their lips, waiting for the producer to pull me early so they could eat up the excess airtime. It was almost as if they could sense the failure. I felt terrible. Not just for myself, but because the producer had started off being so enthusiastic because I was so excitable. She loved the product, and she seemed to like me. But she had a target to hit on that show, and I could tell I wasn't cutting it. I absolutely knew that this producer would now be weighing up 'Do I pull her off early and replace her?' against 'If I pull her off air, where can I find an extra couple of minutes to fill the gap?' against 'Who do I give the extra time to?' and 'Who is going to make me my money this hour?'

I could feel her focus shifting, just as I could feel the punters turning away if I flagged at a trade show back in the day, with Glenda's little rubber stamps. She was doing what the business calls 'chasing the money'. She didn't care that I'd flown out from the other side of the world, that I'd been up for thirty-six hours, that this was my one and only chance. All she cared about was that she now had two or three minutes to play with and hundreds of thousands of dollars to make. If I wasn't going to have made it for her by six minutes, then where was it coming from?

So I've got this very flat producer in my ear, saying 'It's not going well . . .'

I can see it's not going well, pet, I wanted to say. *You reinforcing that in my ear really isn't helping.*

Because I had the live sales figures up on huge screens in front of me, I could see where I was supposed to be and where I actually was in terms of the number of people on the phone. And it was bad. These were enormous, unmissable graphs showing me how many people were on the phone, and how many were on the website, and how many people were buying. And all I could conclude from them was: 'Shit.'

I could see the graphs, and I could hear the negativity in my ear. And all I had left was the determination to stay positive and stay focused. So I did that. I just had to remind myself that card-making was still not a big deal in the US, that no one watching at home knew who I was, and that I would get to the Enveloper soon. I just had to keep going and then surely I could win them round.

About six minutes in, just as I was wondering how much more I had in me, and convinced the producer was now going to pull me, I got to a big reveal. It was like a penny dropped – almost literally. The audience, who had been vaguely uninterested in the cards I had made, suddenly saw the intense satisfaction I got from creating not just a card for a loved one but exactly the right envelope. Perfectly, and to order.

There was an almost instant sense that the penny had dropped for the viewer too, and the little bar chart of how many people were on the phone and on the website started to sky-rocket. I heard the tone of voice change in my ear. 'Oh, okay. This is working, Sara. What you're doing, Sara, it's working. Do more of it.' I picked up a gear and started to make another envelope, my enthusiasm surging as I saw that I was finally getting a response. And all of a sudden, that bloody graph which had been taunting me went from flatlining to a hockey-stick curve, as if by magic.

Say they've got five hundred people in the call centre and you have four hundred on the line, that means your graph is in the black. Once you get eight hundred people on the phone line with three hundred of them on hold, the graph kicks into the red. In a heartbeat my bar chart kicked into the red. So of course the excitement kicks in, for both me and the producer, and I can hear her voice getting lighter and lighter as she encourages me to keep going, to do what I'm doing, to enjoy myself.

Obviously, what happens next is that everything I've learned from the elocution lesson, all the hours of trying to speak slowly, flies out the window, and I get more and more excited, which means faster and faster. To which the voice in my head says, 'Oh my god, Sara, we're killing it now. We're making a fortune, we're gonna run long on the item, keep going!'

So now she's made the decision that I'm doing so well, we're going to eat into someone else's time. I'm going past my seven minutes into eight minutes, into nine minutes, going faster and faster and faster. And we kept going like that until we sold out – which was not that long afterwards. That producer trusted in me, maybe even on a matter of extra seconds, and she made a fortune that night, because we sold well above our planned target for the show.

All I can really remember about what happened next was that I felt as if I was high. It was one of the biggest buzzes of my entire life, let alone my career. I came off the set and I was absolutely wired.

Everyone else was thrilled for me too. I think they sensed how close it had come to going the other way and had got caught up in the excitement of it. When I came off air one of the other guests started chatting to me backstage, saying, 'Oh my god, you are so amazing. That was absolutely brilliant. Do you know there are forums online where people like to talk about all this stuff? You'll be such a hit. I'll show you what they are, if you want to read what everybody's saying about you.'

And like a damn fool I went straight on there. And straight away I learned a lesson about checking online feedback about myself. But there is one comment that has stuck with me for ever and a day: 'Who on earth is this new girl from England? I didn't understand a word she just said, but she was so excited about that product I bought it anyway.'

I just think that pretty much sums up much of my business to this day. I swear the Americans probably still don't understand a lot of what I say. But it's that passion, enthusiasm and excitement that sells. *I'm* excited about my products, because I came up with them. Not only because I invented them but because I know how much the customer is going to love them when they get them home and discover how much joy they bring. And that is visible in any language.

Twelve years later, we are now the biggest supplier of craft products to the TV shopping industry globally, and I personally account for millions of pounds', dollars', euros' worth of sales to many different shopping channels around the world. And that really comes down to the fact that I was so excited about a product I came up with at home with my dad that I couldn't hold it in, even when I was facing disaster.

Chapter 6

What a Rip-off!

———

We had fantastic products. We had cracked America. We were building a strong team. It was almost as if nothing could go wrong, wasn't it? Until it did.

We launched the Ultimate in 2007 and I was at a big UK trade show that year, showing it off. Some guys from Helix came over and started saying how good it looked, how they were big manufacturers of plastic products and how they thought I was great.

Of course, I knew who Helix were. Who didn't grow up with a pair of compasses, a protractor, or even a basic ruler with their name on in their pencil case? They were a staple of everyone's school days! So it was a bit of a thrill to have a big brand name come over, telling me about how they sell into sixty-two countries globally and were interested in becoming a manufacturing partner. Was I interested in that? Might I want to chat? Of course!

I was happy to chat to anybody about anything if it might help me grow my business, and obviously I had a patent for my products, so it wasn't as if they could rip me off. So I went down to Birmingham to meet them, presented the whole concept for the product to their entire team and had a day that I thought was going to be a huge stepping stone for the business. They had even been very interested in the care I had taken over the patent, so I came away feeling safe, but also very excited.

But I never heard anything from any of them ever again. All of the follow-up I did, and they never replied to a thing. Not an email or a phone call – nothing.

By about October of that year I got wind of a new product launching in the craft world. I got wind of it because it was launching on Ideal World. And because it was basically the same concept as the Ultimate but packaged slightly differently. It was called the Helix Craftroom.

I rang the buyer immediately.

'This is a rip-off of my product. Surely you can see it's a rip-off of my product? So why are you going to sell it, and why are you going to let one of your presenters endorse it?'

'Oh no, we have to be impartial,' she said. 'You know,

we just buy the product. We're only involved in that side of it. We didn't make it.'

I understand that attitude now. But let me tell you, I did *not* understand it at the time.

'This is wrong!' was all I could think. 'They've copied my product and I've got a patent on it!'

And my next thought was of Helix: 'This isn't on, I'm going to 'ave 'em.'

The next morning, I spoke to my solicitor, and we began by sending a legal letter to Helix. Off I went, all guns blazing. What I have since learned is that you should never, ever set off on that path unless you are prepared to see it all the way through. What I was absolutely oblivious to that morning, but which I have been painfully aware of ever since, is how much I stood to lose if I lost the case. In short, it could have been everything.

Because once you fire off that first letter, the first thing that rivals can attack you back on is your patent. And the way they do that is to try and invalidate it – so I could have lost my patent altogether, leaving me exposed to anyone, not just Helix. The second thing they do is to operate on a policy that whoever wins has their fees paid by the losing company. This means that if I attack them with that first letter, I'm the one who is starting legal proceedings against them, which means that if I lose, I have to pay all their expenses.

I really did not understand all this at the time. I

understand it all in a lot of detail now, and I paid through the nose for every second of legal advice that taught it to me. And this is why when you see me on *Dragons' Den* I am always the one who asks about all the patents and all the legal side of things.

I know this inside out now. Because I've been through this several times, always successfully. We are always defending our patents, which is why they mean so much to me. Well, that and the fact that the Ultimate patent taught me one of the biggest business lessons ever: how to separate the business from the personal.

I tried to get an injunction out against Helix to stop them launching the product, but they still went ahead and launched it as scheduled. So now I was suing for damages. But what I really cared about was stopping them from trading this product by January, as that was when they were planning to launch it in the US, at that year's CHA show. I was desperate to protect our business there, and suing for damages retrospectively is way harder than stopping the launch altogether, so on I went.

I was only twenty-three, and Simon and I had just got married that September, and now we were hardly seeing each other because of the way the business had taken off. On top of that, this legal battle very quickly became all-consuming. It only lasted a couple of months, but my god it taught me a lot about the sharks' end of the pool.

Above left: Me, aged three, with my parents, Frank and Susan, at a wallpaper trade show.

Above right: Early signs?! In my tutu, dreaming of being a dancer, aged six.

Left: How we met: Simon made the runs and I scored them.

Below: Lizzie, Rosie and me, in our university kitchen. We found the odd time to party despite exams and my new business.

Above: The product that started it all: the Enveloper and its original packaging.

Above: The Ultimate Pro and (**below**) packing it up alongside my colleague Leann, a former customer of ours and now my head of product design (and partner in crime).

Left and right: Celebrating success with our international awards – I'm proud to say the first of many!

Family means everything. (**Above**) With Simon on our wedding day in 2007. (**Right**) Cosy nights with my mam and sister. (**Below**) Our new family, 2016.

My mam, dad and Simon came with me to collect my MBE. Talk about cutting it fine – Charlie was born two days later.

Joining the Dragons line-up for Series 17. We're nothing like as fierce off-camera!

Dreams come true. (**Left**) The moment I discovered Aljaž was my *Strictly Come Dancing* partner. (**Above**) Rehearsing our '9–5' quickstep and (**below**) with my proud parents after the show.

Right: Foxtrotting our way to the top of the leaderboard.

All in a day: crafting; with the family; the glamorous side of business!

Helix's first response to my starting action was basically to bully me. They did not want to go to court, so they began with heavy-hitting legal letters of their own. Obviously, they had large corporate lawyers, whereas I was still using a small local firm that I knew, because I had never had any problems previously. Helix were old hands.

The letters were terrifying, pointing out at a high level why they felt they hadn't infringed my patent. Then they started to try and say why my patent shouldn't have been granted in the first place. I had barely had a chance to draw breath and I was in a double-or-quits situation.

Patent law does not work the way I had assumed it did back then. Patent law is not about who's right and who's wrong. A patent can be invalidated if it can be proved that it wasn't an inventive step, or that someone else has done something similar to you, that you didn't invent the concept.

I had a good patent, I knew that our patent lawyer had done enough work so that these things had been true when it was written. The lawyer who had written it is the same woman who does all my patent work today, including with entrepreneurs from *Dragons' Den*. But all Helix had had to do was to understand *everything* about my product and my patent and then design *around* it in a legal sense. Anybody could see that it was a direct rip-off, but it's not about whether it's a direct rip-off.

My patent is all about the envelope-making. The crucial lines are about 'an abutting edge on a planar surface at 45 degrees to the abutting angle'. Helix had tried to overcome this by using two circular pegs between which the piece of paper, when it lined up against both of them, formed a 45-degree angle. But *technically*, they didn't have a 'raised planar surface at 45 degrees', because they had two points of contact. What they had done was, in a legal sense, very smart. And we could very well have been unsuccessful in defending the patent. But there were a couple of things they hadn't banked on beyond the patent.

The first was my utter naivety. I had only got as deep as I did because I hadn't really taken on board what was at stake until it was too late. There really was a chance that the courts could have decided against us, because of how sneaky Helix had been in pre-emptively being just different enough. The second was that they had massively underestimated the value of the company. In a way, so had I.

The system the courts use is that they estimate my fees (which were put at £150,000), they estimate Helix's fees (which were put at £100,000) and they calculate that to be the cost of the action taken, and then the person taking the action is liable for that cost if they lose the case.

It was very quickly costing me £10,000 a month in lawyers' fees, and this was set to continue if we met in court. Helix had counted on me either being too short of cash or too short of nerves to see this thing through and tried to say to the courts that the case shouldn't even go ahead.

Their argument was that we were such a small company that, if we lost, after we had paid our legal fees there would be no way that we would be able to pay Helix's costs for 'defending' the case. They were saying we would go bankrupt before that so the whole case should be thrown out before it reached the High Court.

By using this tactic of trying to prove that we would go bankrupt, we ended up in mediation. But they had been looking online at our last filed accounts. And because we had started as such a small company, and we were growing so fast, our last filed accounts were eighteen months old. So when they had checked the last available set of accounts and seen a tiny enterprise, they had assumed, 'These chumps are so small, there's no way they can afford to fight us in court.' It was a David and Goliath situation, they had assumed. And it was. Just not the way they thought.

Because we were considerably bigger by now. And I was too far in to back out, so I stunned everyone when I said, 'Fine.' I didn't owe the bank any money, and I didn't need to ask the bank's permission for anything. I could prove on paper that the company had available cash of more than £250,000, and I was prepared to put that amount into a holding account so that we could commit to defending the patent.

It sounds ballsy, doesn't it? But it was terrifying. It all happened so fast, and I had none of the systems in place that I needed to take on a case like this. At one point someone close to the situation – and me – pulled me to one side and said, 'Sara, I think you just need to get some bigger representation. Show them how serious you are. They don't know you, they don't know that you really are serious. Get some big hitters – yes, it's gonna probably cost you twice as much, but you'll frighten them.'

And that's what I had to do. We changed solicitors to someone that was twice the price, just before the mediation, and we scared them witless. But at what a cost! And not just the financial one!

I would sit on phone calls where I knew I was paying the lawyer £295 an hour, and the patent attorney £285 an hour, and the barrister £500-and-something an hour, and every seven minutes I'd hear a little click on the line as we ticked into the next block of charges that would be coming my way.

I didn't understand a bloody word they were saying for the vast majority of the conversations, but I just sat there thinking, 'I'm not going to stop you and ask a question, because I can't afford to hear the answer.'

I was having to go down to London to sit in court to hear what evidence they gave, and then to brief the barrister to give evidence back. I had no experience of this, and I found the whole thing terrifying.

I resented the fact that I used to have to pay for a first-class ticket for my solicitor because he wouldn't travel any other way. Then I had to pay for me to get a first-class ticket too so that I could have a meeting with him on the train, because I was having to pay for his time on the train. These days, I've got the balls to say to a solicitor, 'No, I'm not paying for you to travel first class on the train if that's not how I travel,' whereas back then I just kind of did what I was told.

I just didn't have a Scooby Doo, and I would come home at night and Simon would say, 'What happened? What did they say? And what did our people say in return? What does the barrister think about this?'

I would just sit on the bed and cry, sobbing, 'I just don't know, Simon.'

'What do you mean, you don't know? We spent twenty grand today on that!'

'I just have no clue,' I had to admit. Night after night.

Because I was being led by my emotions, rather than the practicalities of the situation.

As it turns out, while I had the money to fight my case, Helix chose not to and we ended up going to mediation. While I can't go into details as to what was agreed, I was very happy with the result. Helix stopped selling their product as it was and launched a different version of the product which had been tweaked to not conflict with my patent. And it can't have done that well as within a year I saw it being sold off in sale bins in stores up and down the country. Karma is a wonderful thing.

Years later, I was at a trade show and a guy walked on to my stand and introduced himself.

'I worked for Helix,' he told me. 'I just wanted to shake your hand because I've been involved with that company a lot of years, and I think what they did to you was very unethical. You are the first person who has ever stood up to them. And I'm so pleased – even though it was the company I worked for – I was pleased that the case ended up in your favour.'

That was undeniably great to hear. It confirmed what my gut had believed all along. But to this day, I am still not sure that I would behave the same way again. What I had not appreciated when I began the action was how much I stood to lose, and what I didn't understand until long afterwards was just how many people it was affecting.

The biggest thing that I learned about myself from that experience – and it was one that shaped me for ever as a businessperson – was that I had to learn the true meaning of something being 'just business'. My dad at that point was in his fifties and had been in business for thirty-odd years, but he had never made that switch in his thought process. When Helix ripped off our product and tried to bring it to market, my dad was personally devastated. To him, it felt like Mr Helix himself had come up and attacked his little daughter in the school playground. He was an angry, protective dad, even though at that time he was a partner in the business.

He wasn't behaving like it was business, he was behaving like a dad looking out for his daughter. And I was responding with similarly heightened emotion. I felt embarrassed that I had been proud to go in and give Helix that presentation. I felt foolish that I didn't know what the lawyers were saying half the time. And I felt vulnerable because I had played by the rules and only just realized that others might find it easier to bend them.

What I didn't take on board at the time was that nobody made a personal decision to try and hurt me. A board of directors took a strategic business decision that mine was a good product and that my company was too small to be able to fight them in a legal battle. Then they took a calculated risk that they could launch a product which would make their company money. It was nothing personal: nobody knew me as a person. Nobody knew about the nights we had spent wrestling with Battenfeld machines or the hopes Simon and I had for kids or any of that side of my life.

But I responded as if they did, and in doing so I put so much more on the line than made good business sense. I had ten employees by then. And that is a lot of people's mortgages and a lot of children's dinners to be potentially squandering because you have hurt feelings.

It took me a long time to see this. I had to get through the white heat of it, come out the other side, and it was only months later that I could really absorb what had happened. I had a long period of reflection, and the whole experience left me changed as a person.

From that point forward I realized that I cannot let my emotional response to a situation influence the business decisions that I make. If I make a business decision to suit a person or an emotion, and not because it is the overall best thing for the business, I am letting down the now 250 staff who work for me. I am potentially taking a decision for one person that might harm hundreds, and even more if you consider the growth of the business from any further jobs that I might create. Just because that one person, or situation, has an emotional pull, it doesn't mean that I should focus my decision on that if it is not the best thing for the rest of us. So, from that point forward, I took emotion out of making business decisions.

The assumption is that is unusual for a woman in her early twenties to take an unemotional view of business like that, and it is only because I had such a sharp lesson in how the two can become entangled that I developed the skill so young.

It doesn't mean that I don't love my work, or our staff, or our products. And it doesn't mean that I don't also have fantastic friendships with colleagues or business partners. It just means that when I am doing business, I have to do what is best for the company, not for an individual. And it is a skill that I would encourage any young entrepreneur to develop.

Even today, I come across young business owners – on *Dragons' Den* and beyond – who are just too emotional. They have merged their identity into the product; they cannot see business decisions for what they are, rather than as reflections of themselves. There are people who I have mentored and helped to get over the line with this way of thinking. As a mentor or a Dragon, it's up to me to ascertain whether I think they have the mental capacity to cross that line at some point. I don't mind being the one that helps them over it. In some of the businesses, it doesn't matter. But with some it really does.

There are others who I have stopped working with because I didn't think they would ever be able to separate the two. I don't want to be the tough one who breaks their heart, but I also need to protect the rest of my time and my interests. It doesn't happen often, but I have sometimes thought, 'I can't do this,' and left it. It's not about being ruthless, or about making a point – it's about being a realist.

The Helix case wasn't only the catalyst for me developing a realist business sense. It was also the catalyst for another huge change in my life, in almost the opposite way, when my husband, Simon, decided to start working with me. I say 'with me', but what I really mean is with Crafter's Companion of course.

It was a couple of months into the Helix case, around Christmas time, when I was becoming overwhelmed by the magnitude of it all. It was becoming increasingly clear that the company was getting too big, too complicated for my skill set. I simply didn't have the experience for an enterprise of the scale and size that Crafter's Companion was quickly becoming. I'm the ideas person, the one who likes to run at a hundred miles an hour, driving things forward further and further – but I don't have enough of an eye for detail to keep up with myself, especially during periods of huge expansion, so the staff are forever running behind me, sweeping up the pieces. My saving grace is the gift of knowing and being prepared to admit to my weakness: the skill that can take you to the next level is knowing what the skills you don't have are, and being open-hearted enough to accept help. Many a business has fallen by the wayside because of this reluctance to admit where your weaknesses lie, and I didn't want to let mine be one of them.

Simon and I had been together for years, and married for a matter of months, but he had always been a big part of the business, even if only informally at first. When I decided I was setting up the business in America, Simon was the one who was doing all the legwork. He used to work evenings and weekends and take time off his own work to come to trade shows with me because I didn't have any staff who could come. He sort of lived the business with me, despite his own career. He used to work out in the Netherlands a lot during the week, so he would often get up at four o'clock on a Monday morning and be on an early-morning flight. I would get into work at nine o'clock and he'd already started his working day in a different country, while still managing a lot of what my business was up to while he was away.

Then one day he came home from work and said, 'I've been through the finances, and I've worked out that as of today we can take £100,000 out of the business and pay our mortgage off, so we can afford to live on £10,000 a year for however long we need to. Because I'm going to quit my job and come and work at Crafter's.'

He didn't ask me, he just made the decision and let me know about it. Now, a lot of people would think that was horrible, that he was taking control away from me, maybe even bossing me around. But what they don't know is that I was absolutely desperate for him to come and work with us, but I was equally desperate not to put pressure on him by trying to persuade him to join the company.

Not because I didn't want him there, but because he already had such a fantastic career, which he was really passionate about. I am all about the ideas, driven by the creativity and the passion of inventing products and owning my own business. Crafter's Companion was my baby.

But Simon was a corporate guy, and even though it mystified me as to why, he absolutely loved it. He was a proper bean counter, very corporate, and really enmeshed in that system. He was on a trajectory to success, and it was a great trajectory. He was working abroad, flying all over Europe several times a month, managing big teams of staff and accountable for multimillion-pound budgets. He was in a suit and tie every day, polished shoes, smart briefcase. So you can see why I was apprehensive about him giving all that up to work in a tiny company down the road with only eight or nine people in it.

He could see that he could make changes for the company, and he could take pressure off me both personally and professionally. He does have an eye for detail, but I have the passion for growth and ideas. With us working together, we could also set ourselves on the path to being able to start a family and engage with those bigger, long-term life goals. He had our future in mind while I was unable to see past the chaos and pain of this court case. So he gave up his fantastic, beloved career to come and make my dreams a reality. And not only did he do that, but he did it without me ever having to ask.

There is part of me that suspects he probably wasn't

that challenged by working at Crafter's for the first three or four years. And who would blame him? He stopped putting a suit on, he stopped shaving, he completely changed as a person. He had only one condition for coming on board.

'The whole point of me doing this is that I'll run the business so you can go and grow the business,' he said. 'So you go and do all the stuff that you're really good at: product development, sales, innovation, driving it all forward. But if you spend all your time looking over my shoulder, second-guessing the decisions I make, it will not achieve anything, because you won't get the time you need to do your side of it. And plus, you'll royally piss me off. Just leave me to get on with it, and you go and do your thing.'

Honestly, to this day, I know barely anything about what he does, and I swear he probably doesn't know half of what I do. But it doesn't matter. Because we learned to separate the business and the personal, and we trust each other. During the day, the only time we see each other is in meetings where we are surrounded by a table full of other people. And we have had to develop a discipline and resilience around talking about work at home. I am the driving force pushing the business forward, and he is running it day to day. And it just works.

We have successfully defended that same patent six times now, and I've never been involved in any of our other bits of litigation. To be honest, these days, we're in litigation regularly, but it all just happens and I don't even know half the time.

I did feel a terrible pressure on my shoulders when we started working this way, though. I so badly didn't want to piss him off, to make him regret his decision, because he had given up so much. He was used to dealing with these massive budgets every day all over Europe, and here he was in this little local company. There was a bit of control I desperately wanted to keep, it being *my* thing, but I knew I had to let that go if I wanted the help. It was only fair!

These days, a lot of the team think it's hilarious that we don't know what the other one does all day; I think people assume we chat about it night and day. The reality is that we are both morning people, but I tend to get up and exercise around 5.30 a.m., while he gets up and showered. He heads into work when I'm back at about 6.15 a.m. and gets a couple of hours of work before the staff start to arrive at around eight o'clock. I get myself ready, get the kids ready and do the school drop-off, getting into the office for around eight too. Some people think me getting in by then is early, but Simon's already been attacking his inbox for hours! That's because once the team's day starts, he doesn't have a moment to himself. His door is open and there is a non-stop parade of people in and out, asking questions or running things by him. Our paths often don't seem to cross until we're back at the dinner table that evening. If we didn't have the same surname, you wouldn't realize we are husband and wife when you work with us – and that's the way it should be in business.

You've got to stick to this sort of separation between home and work selves, though, because I'm sure you'd go mad otherwise. And I am glad that we set these ground rules before the business grew too much, because otherwise we really would be working twenty-four hours a day and driving each other completely round the bend.

We are an international business, and we do a lot of business in America and China, which means a lot of clients and staff over there are working until midnight our time. We have to be available to them for that. So, in some respects, we're always 'on'. Especially so for Simon, who also handles the early mornings and contact with the Far East.

But then, at the same time, the core values that underpin our business are strong, and we are family people. It is not very often you would see me or Simon in the office past 5.30 p.m. Yes, we'll work on an evening, if we have to take a call outside of UK working hours. But that doesn't mean that I expect the rest of my staff to do that. I'll have a call with America at 9 p.m. if needs be, because it's still in their day, but I won't schedule seven o'clock work calls with employees or contacts in the UK. My staff who have professional contact with colleagues in the US or China will sometimes be flexible, but that is made clear to them when they take the job. Everyone else knows that work is work, and family time is family time – for all of us.

If I need someone else to work out of hours, it will be an emergency, as I don't ask it every day. A lot of employers say that they don't expect late-night or early-morning working, but they do – they think that just saying it is enough. You have to actually see it through and treat the people who work for you with respect. We have some middle managers in the business who think it's cool to be online at nine every night and making themselves available all hours, which only serves to make the more junior staff paranoid, thinking it's that sort of business. 'If my boss is available at nine o'clock and I want to be a manager in this business, do I have to be available to everyone at nine o'clock too?'

A lot of work I do with our management team is about *embodying* our core values, not just stating them. Your behaviour filters down through the company. I have to convey to staff that emails at eleven at night are not impressing me, especially if they're either in a management role, or aspiring to a management role. It takes quite a lot of coaching to make someone understand why that's not a good thing, why that won't get them ahead in my business, or win brownie points with the team.

I will admit that it is a different approach to many companies'. But that is why a lot of people love working at my company. I have always maintained that the key thing that makes our business incredibly successful is that I have managed to attract phenomenal people, to train great people and to maintain them. I've had people move halfway across the world to come and work for us, giving up potentially bigger or better-paid jobs elsewhere to relocate to the North-East of England. I have worked hard on my ability to find them, empower them and then make them feel so valued that it has been worth it. The retention we have on our staff is a huge source of pride to me.

But I could only really set about fostering that environment once I had learned to separate business behaviour from personal behaviour. It is an extension of what I learned as a result of that Helix case, and it still serves me today.

Chapter 7

A Change of Attitude

———

Once Simon was working at Crafter's Companion, we decided to throw 110 per cent at the business for a good few years before we started to think about children. Financially, it made complete sense to get ourselves totally settled, so the first thing he did was to renegotiate all our contracts, recosting what we paid all our suppliers and reworking our finances from the ground up. Within the first month of him being there, we saved more money than his annual salary.

We still wanted a bit more stability before we started the commitment of a family, though. It weighed heavy around my neck that Simon had sacrificed so much. We needed to have the business in a stable position, given that both our incomes were reliant on it, before we could think about having children. All in all, the life plan did not have babies in it for quite a while.

There were a couple of other key things going on around that time too. One was that I had been invited on to the board of the CHA, the Craft and Hobby Association. CHA is the US trade board that hosted the shows I had attended in Las Vegas and Anaheim I told you about earlier – the places where I did my early research in order to launch the business over there. I had learned a lot from their seminars, I had done a lot of business through them now, and I felt as if it was time for me to give back a bit.

'You'll get so much more out of it than you put in,' I was assured, and they were right. But not in the way I thought.

It didn't take me long to realize that I had been invited on to a board that was filled with primarily older, white American men – there were a few token women on the board, and they always had one foreign representative to represent the 'rest of the world' so that they looked like a 'global' organization, whereas, in reality, 99 per cent of their focus was just what went on in the US craft market.

I had had a relatively easy ride with the success of my products up until this point and, the Helix case aside, I hadn't had too many rough-and-tumble experiences in the corporate world. But on the board of CHA I had a steep learning curve about commanding the respect of the room and learning to make myself heard. This is not a criticism of anyone on the board personally, more a realization that I was now operating at a new, global level and it was time to adjust my behaviour and preparations accordingly.

I had to learn to present myself in a way that demanded respect. I'm not just talking about how I dressed, although that was a factor. It was clear to me that once they had put on a suit and tie a lot of the men on this board didn't really think at all about how they looked. It was like they all had a uniform – on the whole, businessmen are not second-guessing what people make of their 'look'.

But I wasn't yet confident in myself and in my business experience to just turn up and feel that I was 'enough'. I felt that I needed to turn up and put on whatever hat was needed to be the Sara Davies that was appropriate for that situation. I was never comfortable enough in my own shoes to turn up and be the Sara I wanted to be, so I used to try to work out every situation beforehand, think about what the people attending would expect of me and my behaviour, and then adjust myself to what I felt was right for that.

It was a key feature of how I approached these sorts of boardrooms while I was in my twenties. By the time I reached my thirties, that was the main thing about me that had changed: I had the inner confidence to go and be the person that I was. This only happened two or three years ago, when I started dressing how I felt I wanted to, in bright colours and bold leopard print. These days, I'm quite happy to go on TV in my capacity as a businessperson and, instead of being in a structured business suit in navy blue, to turn up in a bright, spotty dress.

Back then, I was still years from that. Being on a board at this level for the first time, feeling people judge me when they heard my accent, realized how young I was, saw my blonde hair, was draining sometimes. I'm glad I did it at that age, and I'm glad that I achieved a lot for the craft industry in the UK too. But the steepest part of the learning curve at the CHA was working out how to hold my own in a room full of bullish businessmen.

I used to think that what I needed to do was read the room, constantly. And it was exhausting not being myself. Reading the room, re-reading it and adjusting every ounce of my being to suit what I thought would get me the respect I needed within that room started to gnaw at me during those years.

These days, I'll rock up anywhere and just think, 'Sara, you're good enough to be here. So you don't have to try and be something else or somebody else.' And that's the one thing I say when people ask me, 'What could you tell your younger self?' I wish my younger self could have realized earlier in her career that the you that you are is the one that's good enough. And that's the one that people want to be around. Back then, they were lessons I was only just learning.

No matter how challenging I found it at the time, my experience at the CHA was without a doubt worth it. I felt the tentacles of the business reaching further and further into international territories, growing and getting stronger all the time. But what happened the minute things were looking a little calmer and I was starting to gain some confidence? A massive global recession.

This was 2008, right when the business was really taking off in the US, and that's where the economy took it worst. Our business there just stopped growing. We had to make the decision to shut up shop or leave things just ticking over. We chose the latter. I had faith that things would turn around before too long, and we took the opportunity to let the US side of our business sit simmering while we focused on the UK. After a year or so I stopped working for the Home Shopping Network, and after all my hard work abroad it started to feel as if that side of the business was going to be on ice for quite a while. Naturally, my attention turned more to things at home.

Around this time I had a standard medical where the question of long-term contraception came up, which meant thinking about whether we wanted to put off having kids for *another* three years. I sat down with Simon and explained that I didn't want trying for a baby to be this big, agonizing thing that would hang over me for months and months, so perhaps we shouldn't carry on with contraception but at the same time not start trying 'properly'.

Who was I kidding? Obviously, the minute that old implant was out I was secretly guzzling folic acid and checking the calendar. Of course I was. No one ever said I wasn't prepared to give each new project my everything . . .

I want to be really honest with you about this side of my life, because in business at my level – whether it's on television or in the corporate world – there are still a lot of women who feel that they cannot or should not tell the truth about how much help they have or need. And believe me, I need a lot of help, and I know that I am very, very lucky to have it, and to have so much of it from my extended family.

They couldn't help me back when I was trying to get pregnant, though. If anything, the expectation was making the whole situation feel even worse. It just wasn't happening. Nothing. Apart from my weight yo-yoing, which was just confusing for everyone, especially me. I would wait and wait, getting more and more excited and secretive, then my period would arrive and I would be gutted. I would be so upset I'd have a week of binge-eating, as it seemed I had nothing to lose. Then I would be bloated, and feeling fat, and start to convince myself that, as a couple of weeks had passed, I might be pregnant and it wouldn't matter anyway. Then came the anxiety, followed by my period, and then the cycle began again. This went on for about two years, as I rattled towards obesity. It was otherwise a really happy, successful two years, and from the outside it must have looked as if I had everything. And in many ways I did. But there was one big thing missing and I was finding it harder and harder not to talk to anyone about it.

Things came to a head at Christmas in 2012. I had put on a lot of weight and developed quite an unhealthy relationship with food, and this time my period was due on 21 December. It hadn't come, and it hadn't come, so I decided to do a test on the evening of the 22nd, and then on the evening of the 23rd, and although the tests were showing negative, my period still hadn't come so there was that little glimmer of hope.

Christmas morning, I had the whole family over and was cooking for about twenty people. I had this image of me getting my positive test that morning and having this wonderful happy glow all day. Except, an hour or so before everyone was due to arrive, I got my period. I was distraught. I felt enormous. And a failure. I sobbed all morning and just about managed to get a brave face on in time for dinner.

It was a wonderful meal, and I even felt a little cheered about the situation as I looked around and saw how happy everyone was, all together and having the kind of Christmas I had always loved to host.

'Well, that was fabulous, kid,' said my dad. 'I'll be booking in again for next year! The only thing that would make it better next time would be the pitter-patter of tiny little feet!'

'Oh Dad,' I said, swallowing down the tears and holding back a tidal wave of emotions that I had been keeping from the family for a couple of years now. I hated lying about it, but I also didn't want to worry them. 'I keep telling you . . . we're far too busy with the business for any of that just yet.' My standard line was starting to sound less than convincing. After all, Simon and I had been married for five years now and together for even longer.

My cheeks were burning, and my sister had obviously noticed. It hadn't escaped her that I had gained a ton of weight either, because she was round at mine first thing on Boxing Day, saying, 'How about we both start Slimming World together?'

She had signed us both up by the new year, got us the magazines and, after the first week, she was back round at ours, saying, 'Let's get weighed up then. How's your first week been?'

But I had just put on more weight. I was mortified, and burst into tears in the kitchen.

'What's the matter? It's only the first week. And it's the week after Christmas – don't be so hard on yourself,' she said.

'It's not that!' I wailed. 'We've been trying for a baby

for two years now and it's just not happening! All I do is put on weight ...'

What she did next was exactly what I needed. She did not give me a cuddle and say, 'There there, it'll be all right,' heaping a blanket of platitudes on me. She wasn't one of those 'what you need to do is relax' people either. Instead, she looked at me and said, 'Well, this sort of attitude's not going to help yer, is it?'

I was so shocked I stopped crying and started to listen.

'If you're overweight, your body's going to find it harder. And you're in a negative frame of mind. Your body's not in a good place, your head's not in a good place, you need to just stop trying for a while. Forget it. Just take care of yourself for a good while, lose some weight and start trying again in the summer. You're not too old, you're not too young, you're not too anything. Just give yourself a break and leave it for a bit.'

So of course I stopped trying, lost a bit of weight and, now that the pressure was off, I got into a positive frame of mind and then fell pregnant almost without trying at all. With everything else in my life, I'd learned that the harder I worked, the more likely I was to succeed, and it was baffling to me that the one thing I needed to do here was to do less. To give myself a break? It was unthinkable that something so massive could be so out of my control, but the day I saw that double blue line was one of the happiest of my life.

It was a relief for everyone else too – especially Simon, who at times had been quite despairing over how obsessive I had become. I had found it so hard keeping the whole situation to myself, pretending we weren't trying and were just enjoying the business, and my sister was pretty much the only person in my life who could have told it to me straight like that.

A lot of my family, especially my dad, had really fallen for my line about focusing on the business, but in reality I was desperate to be a mother. Having my own business had been a big part of the dream too as, when I was young, my mam had always been the one helping with school sports day and on the school trip, because as she worked with my dad, she had always had the flexibility. And, of course, in the shop it was her and my nana, so if my mam walked me to school, my nana would pick me up, and vice versa. I had grown up with this brilliant model of working women being able to fit the business around the family, and I had always thought, 'One day, that's what I want to do. I want to have a family, I want to have a business and then I want to build the business around the family.'

That independence was the driver for me, but the only difference was that my business got so much bigger than theirs ever did and it has taken a lot more effort to fit it all in.

When our Oliver arrived in December 2013 I decided that I was going to have three months off.

Properly off. I really wanted that experience of being a new mam, doing the classes, the coffee mornings and making the baby friends. I put the structure in the business that I could be out of the office and unavailable for business for three whole months. I came home from the hospital and I did all the mam things. And I absolutely loved it.

The second time around, when our Charlie was born in 2016, I already had some 'mam friends', I knew the ropes, and I didn't feel the need to do all that in quite the same way, so I didn't manage to switch off from work as much. The day after I had Charlie I had the laptop out. I even had to have one of the staff come into the hospital for a meeting with me, because I was in hospital for about ten days after that birth, as it was a more complicated one.

By the time we were at home, my PA would come over to my house and I would sit and breastfeed Charlie while I caught up with what was going on, and I could hand the baby to her while I did some work. We'd even have meetings at the house, which I never did the first time round.

But with Oliver I wanted to have what I had decided was the full motherhood experience. And without me realizing it, that also came with me putting loads of pressure on myself. I struggled to breastfeed and, even though I had read all the literature, there was still that competitive part of me thinking, 'Bollocks – all women must be able to do it. The survival of the human race depended on it.' So I just about managed it, for three months, and it was one of the hardest things I have ever done. Especially the third month . . .

While I was pregnant the first time around, I was approached by QVC America to work with them. A few years had passed and things were starting to pick up across the pond. An amazing opportunity to reboot this side of our business! They wanted me to do a day's training, though, and it could only be done on a Wednesday. And the first show they wanted me on would air on a Thursday. There was no Marissa there, trusting me with some tapes from previous experiences. I absolutely had to do the training, and they also wanted me to do a full week before I was due on air, in case I fluffed it on the Wednesday and wasn't deemed to be up to QVC standards by the next morning.

This would mean ten days away, so when they approached me I said I could only do it once the baby was a few months old. And in the way that it does with newborns, the time seemed to go on for ever while also whizzing by, and before I knew it I was facing the prospect of over a week in a hotel in Philadelphia. No more sunny Florida; QVC were based somewhere altogether rather chillier. March in Pennsylvania means six feet of snow outside, not taking your baby out in the buggy for walks in the sunshine.

Simon came with me for support (and to look after

the baby while I was on air!), but as we left I still felt a queasy mixture of excitement about the next stage of my career and absolute terror about going away with my new baby – and for the sake of only one hour on television. Poor little thing was only three months old, and I can honestly say it was one of the worst trips of my life.

At first I didn't want to take him. I worked out I could fly out for the training, be away fifty-two hours, and then fly out again a week later for another fifty-two hours to do the show. By my calculations, each of these trips would require thirteen bottles of milk, and I just couldn't pump enough at the same time as feeding the baby. I had the electric breast pump, I was drinking water day and night, but there simply wasn't enough water in the world to keep me hydrated enough to achieve that. So if I wanted to carry on breastfeeding, which I saw as really important – a key marker of me being a good mam – the only option was to go to America with my baby. A classic wild-card new-mother decision.

We got over there no problem. The baby fed the whole way – they told me to feed on the way up and on the way back down so his ears didn't pop, and he was perfect. I was bursting with pride and confidence. Then we got off the plane and he just didn't want to feed. We got in the car at the airport, and he was due for a feed and he wouldn't feed. We got to the hotel and he wouldn't feed. We stayed up way past our bedtime, let alone his, pacing the hotel room. He still would not feed.

It was over five hours and he hadn't fed. And he'd been screaming the whole time. I simply couldn't get him to do it. We were stuck in the hotel room, it was freezing cold outside and Simon was going mad, trying to work out how he could help us.

The next day I had the QVC training all day, so then I was up the whole of the night before, expressing, so as to be able to bottle-feed the expressed milk to him, but he just carried on rejecting breastfeeding all day. By day three in America he still would not feed, and by now I physically couldn't express enough to feed him everything he needed. I was a wreck, speaking to the breastfeeding consultant on the phone, in tears, and in the end we had to go and buy him some formula just to get something in him. Anything. I staggered into that pharmacy, almost crawling with tiredness, thinking, 'I am the worst mam ever. I've killed the routine! The sacred routine! And now he's making me pay for it by refusing the breast!' Distraught doesn't even cover it.

When you're that tired, you forget that you made the decisions you did because you thought they were the right ones for you and your baby. That all flies out of the window and you're left heaping blame upon blame on yourself. I was so distressed that I would now have to use not just the dreaded formula but formula from America, where I couldn't have researched it to within an inch of its life to work out what I was giving my baby.

The minute we got home to the North-East I went to see the breastfeeding consultant, who told me that now the baby was used to a bottle the only way I'd get him back on the breast was to not feed him for so long he'd be starving enough to take milk from anything. But I couldn't do it. I felt as if I'd already put him through enough. I already believed I was the worst mam in the world. So for the next three months of my life, I pumped every two hours (day and night), just so that he could get his precious breast milk. It felt almost like a penance, like I had to pay him back for taking him on that stupid trip, even if it had been worth it from a work perspective – after all, the minute HSN had seen us on a rival channel they'd asked me what it would take to go straight back to them.

I used to take my breast pump into work with me and sit there thinking, 'This is my fault. Because I took my baby to America. I should have done what other women do and just had proper time off. Who takes a three-month-old baby to QVC in America just so they can keep breastfeeding? What do I want, a medal?'

I knew that the QVC contract was important for the business, but I never stopped asking myself if it was important enough to put the baby through that. I was trying to balance the livelihoods of several families – those of all our employees – versus the wellbeing of my one and only baby, and on this occasion my sleep-deprived brain was not able to separate work and home life one little bit.

As you can imagine, this is why, by the time I had our Charlie, I was way more relaxed about everything. From pretty much day one he was having combination feeds. If I wanted to go into work for a few hours, he would have formula, rather than me sitting up all night trying to express milk. I could go to my mam's house and say, 'There's the baby and there's the bottle – can I have five hours at work?' And then, at three months old, Charlie refused the boob as well. So this time I took him straight to see a specialist, and it turns out he had a previously undiagnosed posterior tongue-tie, which they rectified with a simple procedure, and he was back feeding that night. Apparently, these things can run in the family, so the nurse concluded this is probably what had been the case with Oliver a few years previously. So it had never been anything to do with going to America! Yet I had spent the best part of four years feeling riddled with guilt about some stupid QVC training day.

That experience of the trip with our Oliver brought home to me how much my separation between work life and personal life had slipped. Of course it had, I was a new mother. But I knew I had to rein it in. I'd always known I didn't want to be one of those mothers who was at the park pushing their kid on the swing and sending emails for ten minutes while the kid was distracted. These days, my big rule is, if I'm with the kids, I'm with the kids. And if I'm at work, I'm at work.

There is a proper system in place now when I need to go over to America for a major TV show on HSN. I'm away for four days, three nights, and I do the whole trip in the shortest amount of time possible. It nearly kills me, having to work all the way through the overnight flight to catch up on the work I've missed while I've been in the States, but it means that when I land back on Friday morning at nine o'clock, it's time for the kids.

When people ask – as they often do – 'How do you have it all? How do you juggle business and family?' I say that you've got to be present in whatever it is you do. For example, when I go to the States to do those big shows, I don't spend the first day feeling guilty about not being with the kids. I have to switch off from the fact that I'm not with them and focus on the TV show I'm going out there to do. But then that means I'm focused on the TV show and not on my other day-to-day work. Which means that, on the flight home, I often have to spend the entire time catching up on the three or four days' worth of work I've missed. It's not as if the rest of the company stops when I'm abroad!

I think many people would get home from a work

trip with four days' worth of emails to catch up on and maybe use up some of their weekend doing it. Or at least with their phone on the other side of the room, glowing ominously at them. But my choice is to forego the night's sleep on my red-eye flight, spend it catching up on the work, so that when I get home I might be exhausted but at least I'm up to date on work and I can really, truly switch off from it for the next couple of days. That is true time with my family, without keeping one eye on a device. Yes, I've sacrificed sleep, but when I am home I'm home, and that really can be mam time.

I developed this system through trial and error, though: once, I took the later flight and cried the whole way to the States because the kids had seen me up and leaving the house and got all upset. If they don't see me physically go, they barely notice I've actually gone. But that one time they did, I paid for it with days of heartache. I can't FaceTime them while I'm away either – they just get upset, I get upset and the whole thing can deteriorate pretty quickly. If we don't do it, they don't really know I'm in America because they're in a great routine anyway. They'll always be with their grandparents or Simon, their life carrying on as usual. They just think Mammy is 'at work', not knowing where exactly in the world 'work' is that week. It's no different from me working late in the office down the road, even when I'm the other side of the world – they just know I'm at work, and I'll be back soon. When they were younger, when they had no understanding of time and time management, it worked well in that they just got used to being with their grandparents, but if they got sight of me 'away', they thought I might stay 'away' for ever.

Again, it's a case of working out clear boundaries, because if you're trying to do both, you'll do neither well. And then you'll be riddled with guilt – as I learned in Philadelphia. I don't want to be less than the best version of myself at work, and nor should I be. I don't want to let the company or the staff down. That is not fair. And what would I achieve anyway by doing that? It's not as if the kids would get any benefit from me 'missing them more from America' or anything like that.

Having said that ... there is an anecdote that has stayed with me for over a decade now, and I am not sure I'll be forgetting it any time soon. A very high-powered businesswoman once told me, when I was still quite young and kids were not on the agenda, that she had gone to the circus with her kids, and they had had the nanny with them too, because that was just the way they ran things. And a clown popped out from hiding somewhere in the big top and her daughter, who was terrified, screamed and jumped straight into the arms of the nanny.

This woman told me the story as a way of reassuring me that it was okay for her kids to form that bond with someone else because that meant she could work and not worry but, as I laughed along, a little part of me died inside. 'This is no good,' I found myself thinking. 'I'm happy that she feels comfortable with her own life, but I am absolutely not having that. No one is going to be more important in my kids' lives than me.' I just could not have been the better woman in a moment like that and even pretended not to mind. I would have been flat-out devastated.

I knew then that I wanted to have kids, well, because I wanted to actually have some kids around. I did not want them to have a primary bond with someone else while I ruled the world. But this is where I have got so lucky. Because I haven't had to rely on a lot of nannies or babysitters, because both my and Simon's parents live very nearby, which means, since the day our Oliver was born, they have played a massive part in bringing them up and caring for them with us.

Simon is an only child, and I think that when I fell pregnant his mam and dad, Val and John, were really worried that they would become second fiddle to my parents in grandparent duties. I suppose it's a natural thing for a daughter to lean more towards her mam at that time, and now that I am a mam of two boys I can completely see why they were anxious that I would gravitate towards my mam, Simon would follow and that would be that. So they moved to the village!

It's not as if they lived miles away before – they were

only ten minutes down the road – but they wanted to be right there so they were front and foremost in our minds when it came to seeing the grandkids and also being on hand to help us. I've always been so conscious of how much amazing help they've given me, so I always try to be conscious that both sets of grandparents see the kids equally too – when they want to!

When our Oliver was only about five weeks old, Simon had to go to a trade show for about nine nights, and the temptation was to ask my mam to move in with me. But I didn't want Val and John to think, 'Oh, here we go, and so it begins . . .' so I asked my mam over for two nights, Val and John over for two nights and my sister over for the rest. They were all probably exhausted by the time Simon got back, but I do know that me and Oliver loved seeing everyone.

Ever since those early days, both sets of our parents have been amazingly hands-on – from holding the fort when we brought a newborn home to cheering them on at football matches while I've been rehearsing for *Strictly*. In the early days, it wasn't unheard of that, if I'd had a bad night with the baby, Simon would ring his mam and dad on his way into work and all I knew of it was when I woke up in the morning and they'd be downstairs, having made breakfast and ready to whisk the baby off for a three-hour walk in the pram.

As time has gone on, Simon's mam and dad have even come out to America with us so that they could stay with the baby for a few hours at a time while I had meetings or went to trade shows with Simon. The two sets of grandparents even organize their holidays around each other now so that there's always someone around to help. It's almost a full-time job just organizing who's going to be where when, but I am so pleased and so grateful that the kids are always with grandparents if they're not with us.

Everything works so well that when we thought about having a third child we realized that we would pretty much definitely have to get a nanny or the grandparents would be worn into the ground. At that point I looked at what we had and could not believe my luck. I've got two healthy kids, four healthy grandparents, and we are all so close both physically and emotionally. Why spoil that dynamic?

So we didn't. We left things as they were, and I am pleased to say that it hasn't just been the best thing for the family but also for the business. When I fell pregnant the first time, I had a company that was full of people who did exactly as I said, and exactly as I did, and did it really well. By the time I had had two maternity leaves, I returned to a company full of people who had learned to think for themselves and get on with it. And that was what fuelled the exponential growth that followed. It sounds daft, but me stepping back from Crafter's Companion those three months after I had Oliver was one of the best things that ever happened to it. Our turnover went from zero to 10 million in the first few years until our Oliver was born. Since then, it has gone up fourfold. And I know for sure that wasn't just my doing.

One example of a risk we took that I might not have taken if I hadn't stepped back was that in 2015 we decided to open up a few Crafter's Companion shops. I know, right, the perfect time to invest in the high street. Bear with me – there was method in the madness! When I first got into crafts in the mid-2000s there were thousands of craft shops all over the country run by passionate hobbyists. Yes, we were in a good time economically, but also the industry was being driven by these people, who were getting more and more people into crafts simply by being there, providing the personal touch.

Then came the recession, and the loss of so many small businesses on the high street. People stopped being converted to craft. Hard-core crafters were still hard-core crafters, but new crafters weren't coming forward. We had to grow our own market, and we needed an aggressive strategy, so we opened the shops. We weren't looking for them to become huge money-spinners paying all our wages, we wanted them simply to grow the crafters. And that is exactly what they were doing, until lockdown. But more of that later.

Another key change that happened around this time was that we brought in Richard Harpin as chairman.

He is another entrepreneur from the North-East. The business he founded was HomeServe, and he is one of the most successful entrepreneurs in the country. A few years ago, he reached a place in his career where he wanted to expand his horizons and do some mentoring and investing – something I can totally identify with now – and had hired someone to find exceptional entrepreneurs who he might work with. And he chose me. It has been brilliant to have that kind of wisdom to turn to and it has certainly given me more confidence as my career beyond Crafter's Companion has branched out.

But it was in 2016 that the thing which had the biggest impact on my confidence occurred: being awarded my MBE. We were in the office one morning when Kamala brought over a letter that she was worried was a hoax. It said I had been 'put forward' to receive an MBE at Buckingham Palace.

'Well, great,' I thought. 'When are they going to let me know if I'm getting one or not?'

It was only when I rang the number on the letter and actually got through to Buckingham Palace that I let myself believe that it wasn't someone fooling around with me. It turned out that if I'd got the letter, I was getting an MBE. The whole 'putting forward' bit was the weird formal way that these people write these things.

They explained that in due course I would be given

a date when I was to go to the palace, and that it would be sometime in the next six months.

For me, that was right around the time our Charlie was due, so I started to feel a bit panicked. Maybe if it was my first child, I'd have thought, 'I'll just wait till I have the baby and go a few months later.' But this time I was prepared for recovering from giving birth and for life with a newborn and I knew that I absolutely did not want to be turning up at Buckingham Palace feeling really fat with leaky boobs and bags under my eyes the size of shopping bags. So I asked them if I could go for the first available date, in the hope that I could get in there before I had the baby – that way, fingers crossed, I might be blooming, unmistakably pregnant, with glowing skin and hair. I could wear a pair of killer heels, look fabulous in the photos and enjoy a last day out before the rigours of a newborn. I was prepared to run the risk of having the baby at the palace rather than turning up with baby sick on my shoulder, drained from lack of sleep and worrying about my feeding times.

And the plan worked! The day itself was wonderful, and our Charlie arrived only two days later. But the part of the whole process which meant the most was when I told my family I was getting the award. I booked a massive dinner with the whole family, knowing that the awards were being announced at midnight, but no one knew what the big occasion was and why they had all been summoned to dinner with us. My mam and dad convinced themselves that the big announcement was going to be that I was having twins!

Then, as the time approached, Simon got up and did a speech. It was only the second time he'd ever done this. The first was at our wedding. It was such a shock to hear him stand up in front of everyone who mattered to us and say how proud he was of me, how well I had done. He's not a big declarer of his feelings, and this felt immense. And it wasn't just me – everyone was crying with the emotion of it, and no one more than my dad. When Simon finally announced that I was receiving an award, and what it was, it was without doubt one of the top three moments of my life. I could never have imagined such a dream would come true, and so quickly.

Getting an award from the Queen was always one of my career ambitions, but it had always been filed as a lifetime ambition. I thought I might get there in my fifties or sixties. Honestly, I thought I was still a good thirty years away from a letter like that. And to this day, I still have no idea who nominated me. It turns out it's quite a process to do this for someone – a lot of paperwork. And every time I ask someone they say, 'Well, yeah, I would have done it, but I thought you were way too young.'

I had assumed the same, but I think it was because I had always been a little bit self-conscious about being the youngest one in the room. I had come across the implication that I was 'too young' for something important more than once along the way. But I had *experience*. Some entrepreneurs don't get started until they're in their late thirties. There were people twenty years older than me who didn't have close to my level of experience. And something was about to come my way that would make me see that from a whole new perspective.

Chapter 8

There Be Dragons

About a year after being awarded my MBE, Simon and I had some friends round for dinner – Raman Sehgal and his wife and their kids. It was a Saturday night and *Strictly* was on, and I was saying how much I longed to do it. Simon had heard this so many times before that I'm not sure he was even listening, but Raman was paying attention because he was doing my PR at the time. He had a company for pharmaceutical PR and Crafter's Companion PR was a bit of a white elephant for him, but we had been friends a long time so he did the work as much as a favour for me as for business reasons.

'I'm not being funny, pet, but you need to be a bit more A-list than going on shopping telly from time to time before you get invited on *Strictly*,' he said with a smile. Then there was a pause. I could almost see the cogs whirring as he mentally scanned my CV, including the work I had done a few years ago in a female investment group in the North-East called Gabriel Investors. I had been finding it really stimulating and had started to try and take on more and more projects that would give a bit back to the community.

'What about *Dragons' Den*, though? Deborah Meaden was on *Strictly* a few years ago …'

Like *Strictly*, of course that was something I had always wanted to do. I had read all the books written by the Dragons when I was a student and starting out with my business. And when we realized we had moved on to the same street as Duncan Bannatyne there was always a part of me that daydreamed that one day we'd bump into each other putting the bins out and he'd promise to introduce me to the *Dragons' Den* producers. But, as with the MBE, my assumptions about myself and my age hadn't let my dreams get any further than 'Oooh, you're way too young for that.'

I explained my thinking to Raman, who reiterated that I had a lot of experience in business.

'And it's not like you've never done any investing,' he went on, citing my Gabriel investing work.

When he put it like that, I began to see that he was right.

Once Raman had put these things together, I saw how much I had enjoyed starting to mentor people.

Being mentored myself had always been such a huge benefit to me, whether it was Richard at Business Link back in the day or our chairman, Richard Harpin. And then there were all the women, like Deborah Meaden herself, who had inspired me and made me realize there was a place for me in business.

What could I lose by asking Raman to throw my hat into the ring? It was like the women's cricket club at uni all over again. What was the worst that could happen? I'd end up *not* being on *Dragons' Den*? 'Well, that was the case anyway, so let's just give it a go,' I thought. 'It might be a fun project in a few years' time . . .'

The next morning, unbeknownst to me, Raman went through the application process online as though he were applying to be a business on the show, got through to one of the research producers and proceeded to tell them all about me and my potential as a Dragon. And the team from the BBC were interested in having a chat about it. It wasn't too long before one of the researchers called me personally, and then I had a two-hour Skype interview. This was in the days before we all lived on Zoom, so the endless video interviews with executive producers down in London felt very high-tech. What I wasn't expecting was that although they seemed to be very interested, they also seemed to be spending most of their time trying to talk me out of it.

They were basically trying to show me all the

negatives about having a role on prime-time television. 'Have you thought about this?' 'Have you thought about that?' 'How does your family feel?' 'And how do you feel about what they feel?'

What they didn't want was either someone who just wanted to get on the telly and be famous, or someone who just wanted to make investments and would find the telly side of it a huge encumbrance.

This was just before Christmas 2018, and it felt as if they were never going to stop trying to talk me out of it. In the end, they asked me to go away and talk to my family about it over Christmas, to see if I really did want to do it. And if I did, the next stage would be to come down to London for an interview. 'Fine,' I thought.

But when I talked to the family, none of them were really very keen on me doing it at all. My mam had recently seen Cheryl Cole in the papers for something or other and felt that just because she had been on *The X Factor* for a while, now everyone thought it was okay to sling muck at her, and that if I went on telly it might mean the same for me. My dad was equally unkeen, but he wouldn't say what was bothering him.

Eventually I winkled it out of him that he was worried about our family security. He had got it into his head that appearing on television as 'someone who was wealthy' would put us all at risk.

'There's still going to be a lot of other people out

there who are more famous and way more wealthy than me, Dad,' I tried to explain.

Simon was the hardest to bring round and, to be fair, his argument was not unreasonable.

'I just don't get why we need it. I don't get why we want our family in the public eye. There is no benefit to us in being famous, and neither of us has ever been in pursuit of celebrity.'

He was right. We don't exactly pursue a high-profile celebrity lifestyle. And on top of that, it would mean that we were exposing the kids to a celebrity lifestyle, and that comes with an associated risk, which we really did not want.

To this day, I am very conflicted about the boys appearing in the public eye. I am a big family person, but I agreed with Simon that choosing to be not just an investor but a high-profile investor on a massive show on the BBC would mean exposing my family to risk. But I also really wanted to be a role model, or even just a representation of how the sort of working-class, not privately educated, not stick-thin mam that I am could *also* be a big player in the business world – not just making money but creating opportunity for others and being taken seriously. That was the essence of the appeal for me. To show all the future-mes that it was possible.

Simon and I are very much a partnership. When we don't agree on things, neither one of us will pull rank; we always talk it through until we find some common ground. That Christmas he got to the point where he was saying, 'Okay, I really don't like this, but it is very clear to me how much it means to you. So we will make it work.'

And protecting the children is what we do to make it work. I mean, I'm not someone who immediately started attending a whole load of celebrity events – it is very hard to find paparazzi photographs of me out on the tiles. But the family have stayed out of it altogether. It's just the way we choose to mitigate that risk of disruption – not showing my family in public in the way that many other high-profile families do. That doesn't mean that it isn't a massively difficult balance to strike, though. Because I really want to represent working mothers and women in business, and that takes honesty!

I want to be a positive face for women in the work-place, but I also want to find a way to do it without feeling as if I am somehow selling out my kids. In order to truly represent being a woman and a mother, you have to represent what that entails, and to tell the *whole* truth is to some degree to infringe on your children's privacy.

Some people go on about being a working woman, then they don't admit to any of the reality of it – whether it's the snotty sleepless nights or the endless help you need from other people just to keep the whole show on the road. I don't want to champion the fact that I'm a working woman without 'fessing up to the constant juggling, but I don't want to show everyone the daily chaos of the school run either. You can end up going round and round like a dog trying to find their tail in their basket, trying to find the right line, so I think we just have to keep considering it, all the time.

Once we had had these family discussions, I headed to London for screen tests, and everyone seemed happy, but then the BBC had to do their due diligence on me. In short, they had to check out that everything I had told them about myself was true, and to turn over *every* stone in the process. I knew that I had no skeletons in the closet, but the whole thing took so long I started to wonder if maybe I had done something awful that I had no memory of. I'm pretty much as squeaky clean as they come, so I was pretty sure I hadn't, but they had told me that filming started on 24 April, and when I still hadn't heard anything by the end of March I was really getting tense. In the end, I got the green light.

I had spent so long waiting, and so long debating the downsides of being on the show, that when the first day of filming came it almost felt like a bit of a let-down. Even going to see the wardrobe team made me quite nervous, as I knew it would be back to the same battle of trying to look like myself but trying to look like I should be taken seriously at the same time.

I had assumed a few months earlier that just the thought of being on BBC at prime time would have given me the kick up the ass I needed to lose some weight. But it just didn't. I was clearly comfortable enough in my shape that taking care of myself stopped being a priority. I had had gestational diabetes during both of my pregnancies and I knew I was at a high risk of type-two diabetes. I was told literally as I left the hospital when I was having Charlie, 'You must get your weight under control, otherwise you will go into pre-diabetic range quite quickly.'

Similarly, I have always wanted my kids to have a healthy relationship with food, as mine has not been great at times, and I have also always known that means them seeing me having a healthy relationship with food.

But this stressful waiting meant that I didn't lose any weight for *Dragons' Den*, and although I don't profess to being or want to be the thinnest person, I did want to be healthy. So I took myself off for a Bupa check-up and was told, 'Well, the good news is that you're not in the pre-diabetic range *yet*. However, your BMI is over thirty, so you do need to get it down. Otherwise, if we're having this conversation next year, things might be very different.'

My heart sunk a bit.

'We need to talk about what changes you can make in your life for that to happen,' the doctor continued. 'I think you need to get a personal trainer, because you need some accountability.'

'I've got a personal trainer,' I replied. 'But the problem is he only works between twelve and nine. I can't go during the day when I'm at work, then come home at night, give the kids their tea, put them to bed at eight o'clock – when I quite often fall asleep myself anyway – and then get to the gym for after eight o'clock. I don't think so. My PT sessions are just building up, not getting used.'

'Okay, go in the morning.'

'I can't!' I said. 'Our morning starts at quarter past six. That's what it takes just to get me ready and the kids out of the door for school. There's no time in the morning!'

'Right. Half past five then.' She really had her mind set, this one. 'Just two mornings a week. I'm only asking you to commit to two mornings a week . I want you to find a personal trainer who will be on your doorstep those two mornings a week. And I want you to book in all the sessions from now till Christmas, because it takes three months to form a habit. If you book them, you'll give yourself the accountability, the habit will form and then things will change.'

It was like the time my sister told me to stop feeling sorry for myself about not getting pregnant. I came away feeling empowered, that I really could change things. So I rang the guy who owns the gym – which, incidentally, doesn't open until six o'clock – and begged him to find me a solution. Then I told him that I could *not* be the point of contact for the trainer. I said that any cancellations had to come from Rachel, my PA. So that I could not, ever, decide at nine o'clock at night, 'Nah, I'm not gonna bother tomorrow,' and roll over to sleep the next morning. It had to be cancelled by Rachel, and even then just moved to a different day. I decided to prepay (knowing how tight I was, that would surely make me get up!), and that I could not cancel. And guess what? I didn't cancel. Within three months, the habit had formed.

Making this commitment to getting fit was one of the best decisions I ever made. It was prompted by me starting to appear on TV, but the benefits went far beyond anything the viewers might have seen on screen. I finally found I did have the willpower to get up and out of the house to exercise, and I discovered how much better it made me feel and how far the positive impact on the rest of my life reached. Particularly when lockdown came around and I had finally learned that you didn't have to be good at a sport to enjoy getting fit. It was a lifesaver, in more ways than one.

I didn't know all that on my first day of filming, though, and I was nervous as hell to meet the other Dragons, especially Peter and Deborah. They had certainly been two of the mentors who had not known they had mentored me. I had read their books, taken in what they had to teach me, followed their progress, the lot. They meant so much that the thought of falling flat on my face in front of them – financially or physically – was terrifying! Once I had met them and we were all sitting there, shoulder to shoulder, waiting for that first entrepreneur to appear, I felt as if I had finally earned my status as a Dragon. And despite my nerves, they could not have been more charming!

What I hadn't anticipated about the filming day was how little the Dragons are told ahead of time. The good thing about the studios is that there are two separate entrances for the Dragons and the entrepreneurs, so we aren't even in the same part of the building as them – we can't accidentally bump into them in Make-up or anything. We come in and head to our dressing rooms, where we get changed. Once we're ready, we go and sit in the chairs, and there are huge black screens in front of us. The team do our hair and make-up touch-ups and check the sound, then the director gets a note from the floor manager and calls out, 'Entrepreneur in the lift!' It's only at this point, when the entrepreneur is heading up, that they lift the screens out of the way and we see the product they're pitching for the first time.

Some people don't seem to believe that we really don't see anything beforehand. But we don't. That's the whole point – what you're seeing on television are our real reactions. We're not actors – we would all be terrible actors! Even when we have to pick up some extra lines at the end, if one or two of us might have spoken over each other, we are all terrible at it, so completely stilted and useless at faking a repeat of our genuine reactions. It is, every time, the biggest nightmare of the day because, as you can imagine, none of us are very good at pretending, or being asked to repeat ourselves again and again.

While I'm telling you about behind-the-scenes at the show, I suppose you want to know what we are *really* looking for in our investments. I can't speak for any of the others, but I suspect what they're looking for isn't too dissimilar. These days, I have a choice between investing my personal wealth in my own business, where I can control what happens to it every day, or investing my personal wealth in other people's businesses. On the one hand, I have total confidence that if I'm investing in my own company, I can control where that money goes and be pretty reassured that I will get a solid return on that investment. On the other hand, I cannot micromanage every business I invest in, and I accept that I do not have as much confidence in someone else making me the money as I do in myself.

However, what I get from investing in others is entirely different from what I get from investing in my own company. There's only so much personal fulfilment I can get from my own business. And I don't just want to get a fluffy, philanthropic fulfilment from being a mentor, because I genuinely believe that people don't appreciate things that they get for free. So I feel that if you bring me on board as an investor in your business, you are getting me – and I come at a price, which is giving up a slice of your business, but then you also get a fair value for that financially. Yes, I am giving you my money, but I am putting a part of myself into the business too. And I know that little part of myself is worth way more to you than my money will ever be.

My time is in far more limited supply than my money at this stage in my career. So I've always known that what I am looking for is *more* than an investment to make my fortune. It has to be an investment that can enrich my life in other ways – something that is interesting as well as profitable, or something that does social good as well as breaking even.

So I have to be really selective in the businesses I choose to give *myself* to, because the main credential is not always deciding which business is going to give me the greatest return on investment in pounds. It needs to answer the questions: What am I personally going to get out of this relationship? Am I going to develop as an investor or a mentor? Am I going to get personal satisfaction from seeing that person develop, having a relationship with me?

These are all the plates I have spinning in my head as I am sitting there in the Den. I think that what really sets me apart is that I have chosen *not* to make offers on some entrepreneurs, even though they could be multimillion-pound prospects. I just know I will not get any personal fulfilment from investing in that business.

I'm not 'in it for the money'; if anything, I'm in it for *more* than the money.

When I look at the proposed businesses, I'm thinking not just 'How much money could you lose or make me?' but 'Can I really work with you?' Sure, you might be able to make me millions, but I can do that myself. What I can't do is find interesting people with stimulating ideas – I need you for that. This means that, when I'm considering your business, I have to feel like you're the sort of person who can learn from me and be willing to learn from me and enjoy that.

I have made investments in the Den where I maybe don't have an overly great interest in the product itself but I do really and truly believe in the entrepreneur and I can see how much they can learn from me. In those cases, where I know I will enjoy giving a bit of myself to them, and watching their journey as a result, other people might be wondering what on earth I'm seeing that they aren't ... but that's where the fun is, isn't it?

I would say that a tip that I would give anybody who was coming into the Den is that I am well aware of the fact that you can train anybody to say anything. You could train someone to go in and deliver a really compelling performance in a job interview. But, as when I'm interviewing someone for a job, I have to be able to look past the big talk and the facade and at the real person. It's up to me to probe with questions that will get me to the real person, not rely on whatever script that person has learned to deliver in that situation.

The probing questions are not intended for me to just turn over the stones of 'Do you know your business? Because you should know your business.' I need to get to know you and understand you as a person to make a decision on whether, emotionally, I'm prepared to invest in *you*. Give you a bit of *me*, not just my money.

One thing I have always, always, been really strict on, though, is patents. As you can well imagine, I do not want any of my entrepreneurs to go through what I had to go through in the Helix case. Quite often, if I'm thinking, 'I might go for this one,' and they're telling me their patent is watertight, I'll say, 'I'll look at the paperwork and decide for myself, thank you.' It only took one series for the other Dragons to get me to take a look at the paperwork if they're interested in investing in something. And that made me feel really great! Because the other Dragons have way more years of business experience, of investment experience, of life experience, but they know that I have some great experience of my own. (And the reason they know is because I regaled them with the full Helix story over dinner one night, with hands flying and a couple of bottles of red wine at the ready . . .)

Nothing makes my heart sink more than someone

telling me, 'Oh, we've got a worldwide patent,' because the immediate answer will be 'Well, you haven't got a worldwide patent, pet, because there's no such thing. So where have you *really* got your patent? Where was it granted? What was your filing date? Have you put your PCT application in? And can you just give me the first line of your claims?' When you start to get the 'eerrrr' back, you know they're screwed.

Because it's one thing to have a patent and, as we know, it's another thing to be prepared to defend that patent. I'm often trying to weigh up how strong their patent is, if they have one. And if they've got to go and defend that patent, what is the price they potentially have to pay if they lose it? What is their appetite for doing that? And could I do it alongside them in a helpful way?

The same woman who did my first-ever patent meeting with me, sixteen years ago, who helped me with my Enveloper patent, is still with me. These days, when I do a deal in the Den, before I even personally speak to the entrepreneurs to take it to the next level, I'll have her interview them and basically give them and their patent the once-over.

I've already had a case whereby someone thought they'd got a patent but, actually, when we went into detail in the paperwork, they'd missed a filing date, which rendered their whole application null and void. The thing with patents is that it's so critical to get it right, because you can't go back and put it right after the fact.

It really is the worst feeling in the world when you ask somebody who has a brilliant idea – and it's become clear that it's completely unique – 'Do you have a patent?' and they say, 'No, but I'm going to apply for one soon because there's nothing like this.' You know in that instant that they now can't get a patent because the very fact that they have told production staff, camerapeople and a row of Dragons their brilliant idea means they now cannot apply for that patent. You just can't do it retrospectively! Otherwise, everyone would be trying to patent every idea they heard their mates bragging about at the pub, or every time investors had a meeting with someone they could just patent the good ideas when the person left the room!

It has certainly not been all frustration, though. I have made some fantastic investments and met some fantastic people. A real favourite has been Helen from EasyTots, which is totally my wheelhouse. Her products are silicone bowls for kiddies which suction on to highchairs so your little one can't start lobbing your purées over the side the minute you set the food down in front of them. Which, of course, anyone who has been a mam knows is their favourite game in the world.

What really impressed me about Helen was not just that she had a great product, which she had come up with by solving a problem she'd spotted, the same way that I had – but that she had really, really done her research. She had learned everything there was to know about the Amazon algorithm, she had worked out how to sell her product really well, and while she might not have had the most experience in the world, she had the sort of savvy that meant I knew I could really help her along. She's got such drive and determination, and is a really great businessperson who I so wanted to work with and am thrilled that I could.

Another one is Kameese from Nylah's Naturals. In her I saw a fantastic storyteller and, again, that was something I knew from personal experience was a huge part of the package. She invented a product for Afro hair. Her daughter had Afro hair and aggressive eczema so she didn't like putting a ton of chemicals on to her scalp. So Kameese ended up researching and researching until she worked out how to make her own vegan haircare products. On the kitchen table! Out of only natural ingredients! Because it was working so well, she started mass-producing them for others, then wanted to find a way to bring them to market.

She's a Black single parent, and she came on *Dragons' Den* because she just didn't have the experience or training to know how to take the business to the next level, or how to meet people like us through any other avenue. My challenge when I was looking at her product was that it is a niche, a small niche of the market, and difficult to grow. But I'm used to being in a niche industry – crafts – and I know a lot of people probably find what I do really dull. But then, if you had had the opportunity to invest in my business when it was tiny, you'd be a multimillionaire by now. So I've got that unique kind of take on it. I know what a niche business can do, so I'm not prejudiced about them.

So I figured that was not worth dwelling on. Kameese also has such incredible drive and determination, and I could see that, yeah, I don't think she's going to be the one that makes me millions – because the size of her market is limited – but it is still a valid business. There is still a great market for the product, and she just wants her product taken to market and given the best possible chance with the best possible team.

The sheer enjoyment I get out of watching her personal journey and knowing that I have played a role in helping her be even more successful than she might otherwise have been is incredible. And the branches will only spread from there, because she in turn will inspire people in her community to try their ideas, and so on and so on.

I don't want you to think that I sit behind those black screens of a morning, thinking, 'Oh, please be a woman.' I have obviously done other investments that aren't like the ones above, and some are going to be great as they come to fruition over the next year or so. A good example is Willsow, for whom I had to fight off the other Dragons. These are kids' books made with special handmade paper embedded with seeds, so you read the book then plant it! And over the following weeks, you and your kids or grandchildren watch as what you learned about together comes to life.

I wanted it so badly, for two main reasons. One is that, as a mother, I could see that it could really teach my kids about something meaningful in a way I thought they would interact with. I understood that product first-hand as a potential consumer. And the other reason was that it wasn't just about how much money the business could make me, it was the fact that they were doing something good for the world with the business. That's what I like to be able to do. I don't want businesses that are just doing good but aren't commercial, but these guys could make money while really teaching young kids about where their food comes from. It was also a second-generation family business of printers in an industry that was struggling a little bit, but they'd really thought outside the box of how to get out there and do something different, make something of that business by being brave.

My heart and soul are in the businesses where I know that I can make a real difference. I was the investor for them, and we found each other. I didn't join *Dragons' Den* to be a magpie, picking up the pretty shiny things here and there where they caught my fancy.

The problem is that you also get *some* people who

will not be told otherwise. They believe that their product is the best thing since sliced bread, and all that they've heard from friends and family is it's the best thing since sliced bread. You can tell from the moment they walk in that even if you say to them, 'I'm sorry, mate, but that is a load of rubbish,' they will just say, 'Nah, what do you know?' They're just not going to hear it.

The other awful moments are when you get people who are sharing their dreams. And you know that you will be shattering them if you say what they don't want to hear. Even if you think the idea or the product is good but you just don't think you're the right person to partner with them, you still can't take it on because you're feeling too 'kind' to say no to someone. Because it wouldn't be kind to say yes to a fit that you knew, in the pit of your stomach, wasn't quite right.

My time on the show has not just been about the investments, though, I have made genuine friendships with the other Dragons too. Touker Suleyman, in particular, became an instant real-life mentor. I had done my screen test with him, so on that big first morning he was the only one that I'd met beforehand. And he instantly felt like my uncle. He's a very warm, endearing, approachable man, so I wasn't nervous at all about meeting him again. As I've done many times in my career – it was something I learned to do a lot with the guys who were on the CHA board of directors, for example – I went up to him on my first morning, and I said, 'All right, Touker, just to let you know, I've decided that you're going to mentor me through this.'

I told him straight up that this is what he was doing, and admitted that I'd done investments before but not this high profile and I wanted to learn from him. 'I need a lot of help. This is my first time doing anything like this at this sort of level, but I've decided that you're the person to help me with the rest of it.'

I could just tell he was the sort of person who would take really, really well to me saying that. And I saw his chest puff out a little bit when I did. He looked so chuffed, and he really took it seriously – especially because he was sat in the chair next to me. All the way through the day, he would give me little tidbits, tips, pep talks. He even offered to come in and split my first few investments with me 50:50 so that he could then help me through the next stage of the process, which was the due diligence on the entrepreneur. He really has treated me so well, I'm so glad I put it out there from day one that I needed the help. I haven't just been dispensing knowledge on the show, I have been gaining it too.

Touker is far from the only Dragon who has shaped my business experience, though. I have also learned from Deborah, who has been flying the flag for women in business way longer than I have. She has forged paths that have made my journey smoother, from being a high-profile woman in business to one who consistently speaks out for them. I have definitely employed my fair share of women over the years, but I have done it by genuinely hiring the best person for the job each time, and a lot of the time it has happened to be a woman. I guess I just saw something in a lot of younger women that maybe men in business might not. My attitude is that I want to keep talking about my positive experiences so that young women who don't have the kind of family support that I had can see that there is a path in business for them, that it won't be lonely in there, as there will be people like myself who are thriving. I relish the chance to use my profile on TV to be a role model to any would-be entrepreneurs out there watching – particularly any young girls who might not see elsewhere that, in business, being ordinary can also be enough.

Because she was in business for years before me, I feel that Deborah has had to take a different approach. On that very first day in the Den, my first-ever pitch was a street-food stand they had parked up in the Den. They wanted us all to get up and queue for some street food and then sit back down and eat it in our chairs while the pitch was going on. Touker got up before me and went over to this street-food wagon, and I said, 'Oh, come on. Ladies first . . . ladies first.'

I'm quite old-fashioned like that. Chivalry is a big

thing for me, and I am not ashamed of that. But Deborah barked at me from behind, 'None of that in here, thank you. We're not "ladies and gentlemen". We're all just Dragons. And we're all the same.'

She was quite quick to get that in from the very beginning. Literally minute one, of pitch one, on day one. She was making sure she made her mark, and that is because she must have spent years and years fighting to get that level of respect, to reach that point where she could make statements like that out loud and not face reproach.

I could almost feel her thinking, 'I'm not having this young lass come in here and set me back years,' and to be honest, I don't blame her. She was straightforward about it, like she is about everything. She has been an absolute icon but has managed to do it while also being incredibly kind to me, supporting me through my first year on *Dragons' Den* with advice, texts and calls, and then going on to do it all over again when I followed in her footsteps on to *Strictly*.

Working with Peter Jones and Theo Paphitis has also been like a dream come true for me. I used to watch them in awe when I was at university, and I told that to Peter on my first day, thinking he would be thrilled to know that he was basically a key part of my growing up. I'm sure he *was* thrilled – but he also told me to shut up for making him feel so old!

I had honestly been learning from him for over a decade, though. He was one of those mentors of my past I talked about, the ones who never know they're mentoring you … until I made the mistake of telling him! Just as I used to sit and watch during all those CHA meetings at the start of my career, assessing who was commanding the room, who I had the most respect for, and why, I have long modelled myself on how Peter behaves in the Den, and now I get to do it in the Den myself. I honestly have to pinch myself sometimes when I realize that I really am sitting alongside him on the panel, co-investing in businesses with him, Tej and the others.

Theo is not a permanent fixture as one of the Dragons these days, but I have shared a similar dynamic with him as I have with Peter. I have also sought his counsel beyond the show, and we have become good friends. Whenever I've had to make a huge business decision, I've taken him out for a nice dinner, chewed his ear off for a few hours and come home with a load of free business advice.

If only my own children could be as impressed by *Dragons' Den* as I was. They could not have been more disappointed when the first show finally aired.

'Mam,' said our Oliver, looking round. 'We thought you were going to be a dragon. You don't look much like a dragon in that spotty dress. And where's the den?'

Little did they know that I was only a couple of years away from playing the Mother of Dragons on Saturday-night prime time. But before that, there was the small matter of a pandemic to get through.

Chapter 9

Surviving a Pandemic

———

I don't think it would be fair to tell you about the challenges I have faced as a business leader without talking about the pandemic, lockdown and how we responded to those challenges. It was a horrible time for everyone and it tested my skills as a businesswoman, a boss and a mother to the absolute max.

Like most business owners, at Crafter's Companion we had an idea that something was going to happen for a few weeks, but no one understood what it would be. The States went into lockdown, Italy was in full lockdown, and of course we had been watching China since the beginning of the year. It was looking inevitable that the UK would head into some sort of lockdown sooner or later. But we had no idea what any of this would mean for our organization, or whether we would survive at all. All we knew was that if the warehouse had to close, if we couldn't ship anything, then we wouldn't be able to make any sales and so we wouldn't be able to pay staff wages. This was long before any talk of furlough schemes – none of us had even heard the word! – so when we tried to make a plan for lockdown, we were really starting on a doomsday footing.

Businesswise, preparing for the worst seemed like the only sensible thing to do; we really did not know if the business was going to have to close its doors altogether. On a personal level, at that point, none of us knew how vulnerable we really were. My dad has COPD (chronic obstructive pulmonary disease), all four of the grandparents were told they would have to isolate, and there was very little information back then about how that protection would work or what the implications were.

When the lockdown was finally announced, we understood quickly that all our shops would be closing, and that all the stores we supplied would be closed too. All the local independents, all the impulse buying – gone in a heartbeat, and for who knows how long. Our wholesale business would grind to an immediate halt.

What we didn't know was if our warehouse would be forced to close; if it was expected to close its doors, the whole business would be grinding to a halt, which in turn meant we didn't know if the business could survive. For someone who likes control and positivity, it was a challenge.

Our business is categorized as a 'multi-channel business', which basically means that we sell product into lots of different channels of sales (directly to the consumer through our own stores and website, wholesale through little independent stores or big multinationals, through the TV channels and through marketplaces such as Amazon). Some of those channels were switched off overnight but, thankfully, the government launched the furlough scheme, which meant that any of our staff who were working in stores or on the wholesale part of our business were supported while they couldn't work.

Over the coming days, as details of the lockdown were outlined by the government, we worked out that the other channels (TV shopping and ecommerce) could continue trading, and my challenge was to look for ways to drive those areas of the business forward to hopefully make up for the shortfall we were seeing from the other areas. We could at last start to see a semblance of a way forward, but it seemed like every business – and everyone – was responding differently to the situation. We knew we had to act fast, but I didn't want to act impulsively.

That first day of lockdown, the Monday on which the prime minister gave his first address to the country.

I stood in the middle of the office and addressed the staff. I sellotaped my phone to the railing beside where I was standing, making a Skype call set up to address the staff who were working remotely at the same time as those still in the office. I was stood there, staring at all the uncertain faces in the little tiles on the screen, then looking up at the sea of bleak faces across the room, and I realized how much everyone was depending on me.

I could see that everyone was scared – very scared. Worried about the unknown – worried about their health, their family's health and their livelihoods. I was too. And they were looking at me for all the answers. And I stood there and just explained what was going on – and what I intended to do in order to protect the company and therefore their jobs. And I had to do it in a way that took into consideration my respect for the hundreds of different personal circumstances a large number of staff would have in this situation.

I didn't really have any notes, just a few scribbles of need-to-know stuff, because the last thing anyone needed was me sounding like a distant corporate figure when what we were all going through was so profoundly human. I told them everything I knew, and all the plans we were putting in place, how we were going to try and keep things running for as long as possible – and how much I cared about making this all work. Most importantly, I was clear about what I didn't know too. It was the most vulnerable I have ever felt: I cried, and a lot of the staff cried with me.

Part of the sadness I was feeling is that I am the most positive person you'll probably ever meet, the eternal optimist. I bring that to the table in every meeting I attend, and I am also Sara the saleswoman – finding the positive spin in every scenario to get everyone on board with whatever it is I'm explaining or selling that day. But in that moment I couldn't be the 'me' that I am best at being. Going out there and painting the picture of optimism would have meant creating false hope, which would have been even more dangerous than raw honesty.

Every part of me was crying out to give the big 'We will be back to normal before you know it!' speech, but it would have been cruel. It would have been the easiest thing in the world, and it would have given me a huge boost, made me feel great in myself and probably would have had everyone in that room cheering and heaving a massive sigh of relief. But I simply could not have guaranteed that what I was promising would come true. Instead, I told everyone at home and in the office that I would work day and night to help us make it through. That they should never worry that I wasn't trying to bring us all out the other side, that they were all being thought of.

I looked over as I was finishing up and saw that Sharon, who had been with me since I stole her from

Graphicus all those years ago, was sobbing her heart out. She knew how much this business meant to me, she knew I was telling the truth about how much I wanted us all to make it. But she was obviously really worried too. I could see what she was going through, and I knew that she could see what I was going through.

After a few days it became clear that the warehouses would not have to close if we could make them safe. Everyone was so relieved and we got on the case with masks and social distancing immediately. I wanted to make a big show that this was positive, that no one who felt unsafe should have to feel unsafe. Car-sharing had gone from being encouraged to being banned. None of us complained about the annoyance of having a mask on all day. We just wanted to get through, together, because we could see that many others might not. Everyone was amazing. My staff were just incredible, and I learned so much about the team we had during this period.

You might think that a lot of people, the ones who were on furlough, would be sitting at home rubbing their hands together with glee at the fact that they were getting 80 per cent of their salary without having to leave the house. But quite quickly what we found was that, on the whole, the staff who were on furlough were often struggling at home because they were overcome with guilt because their colleagues were going into work, and many of them were working twice as hard as usual because they had roles in areas which meant they were keeping a company there for their colleagues to come back to. People were offering to help out, but they weren't allowed by law on the furlough scheme. They literally had to sit at home and do nothing – but instead of it always feeling like a luxury, they were in many cases missing friends, their work family and, most of all, missing their sense of purpose. It was a big lesson in what fantastic staff I had, and it also reaffirmed my thoughts on the therapeutic nature of working hard and getting a job done well.

Seeing this team spirit pushed me even harder to want to keep people in their jobs. When you're a small company with only a dozen staff, you know everybody and everybody's family situation. But when you get to a few hundred staff you can't possibly know everything, so it gets harder to have that emotional connection with every single one of your staff – but a time like this certainly restored my sense of an emotional connection with all of them again.

As a result of this increased connection, I emailed the whole company every night for the first month or so. I used to sit at home of an evening and compose it myself, telling them exactly what we had got on with that day, the little wins we'd had, or any other news. And I would let everyone know I was thinking of them. I used to go down to the warehouse every week and walk around and speak to all the staff personally, thank them individually for how hard they were working, reassuring them that what they were doing was basically securing the long-term future of the company. And after a month or so, I spent a day sitting at home, handwriting a card to every one of the staff and sending them a little bar of chocolate to say that we were thinking of them. It took me a while, but I got those hundred and fifty cards out. I knew enough about the personal situation of each person – whether it was wishing them solidarity with homeschooling or sending best wishes to an elderly parent – to write something individual in each one, before popping a little bar of Dairy Milk from the box on my desk into each envelope. I told the staff who were still working so hard how much it meant to me, and I let all the staff on furlough know that we were thinking of them and missing them.

I look back on those first few months with a strange sense of fondness now. We all discovered new parts of ourselves and saw value in the people around us that we might not have seen before. I saw so many of my staff step up to the plate in a way I've never seen them do before, everyone rallying round. All the petty little things that used to bother people went out the window. This golden period only lasted a couple of months, mind, but we did it.

Then there was of course the small matter of running a household with the schools closed as well. Like many mothers out there, I learned quite quickly that I was not cut out for home-schooling. Most days, the three of us would be crying by lunchtime. In those first early weeks, Simon would head into work in the morning to take care of things and I used to try and work from home and look after the kids. Then Simon would come home and look after the kids for the afternoon and I would go into the office. As far as home-schooling goes, I think it is a case of least said, soonest mended – and thank heavens for childcare bubbles coming along as soon as they did!

The days were so full-on that I knew I had to carve myself a little space in them, so I would get up between five and five-thirty and go for a run. It was my way of coping with the panic. Just that hour or so to myself, running around, feeling free. I used to climb over the fence of the golf course near where we live and run around the course, feeling so peaceful, so glad to have this little slice of time to wrap my head around the magnitude of what was going on – not just for me, or us, but globally.

It had been such a big thing for me that I had got into the habit of running at all, and now I found myself able to keep it up even without the personal trainer. I would just get up and go. Then, because I found it was so helpful having that time to myself, my time to think, I started getting up earlier and earlier. As it was summer and the mornings were light, sometimes I was up as early as 4.30 a.m. I couldn't believe it myself.

I would just go and go, further and further distances, my brain firing on all cylinders. I mean, it wasn't as if we were ever having any late nights, as there was nothing to do and nowhere to go. So I was awake super-early every morning, but I still had a good seven hours' sleep. I couldn't wait to get into work – I'd be driving in, ringing the staff who were working from home, downloading all my ideas on to them. Every day I was full of new plans and new inspiration – it kind of took me back to my really early days in the business, being the ideas woman, leaving her trail of mayhem behind her!

Having said that, I do think the staff found it motivating that I was so positive and so full of ideas. Not every one of my hare-brained ideas worked, but I had so many of them that every morning we were in with a shot of getting some to pan out okay.

I would think everything through on those runs, and I really do think they were a huge part of holding my sanity together. How was I going to be the smiling face of the company if I was spiralling with worry myself?

Once we had our basic systems up and running lockdown-style, I had the mental space to look at what I could do on a practical level to maintain both sales and morale. My biggest skill is selling products on television, so we decided to ramp up a concept called Crafter's TV that we had initiated a few months before the pandemic started. We started it because we were doing all this TV shopping, but we realized that, especially in America, our customers wanted to take a whole class in learning how to use things once they'd bought them. So we were doing these extra educational-content shows to teach people how to use our products: because we're a multi-channel retailer, you could have bought that product anywhere, and in lots of cases it had not been bought via shopping TV, so the customer had never seen me demonstrate it and had no idea that I did that. It was time to show them! First of all on Facebook, then on YouTube. It started off as a way to support our other sales channels, but it actually became the star of the pandemic for us.

It was all back to the essence of what made us unique as a business proposition – education and demon-strable products – because all the products we sell are designed to be useful rather than (or sometimes as well as) stunning to look at. So if you don't know how to use them, how tempted will you be? But if you're a crafter on a forum, unable to leave the house at a time of high anxiety, of course you're looking for ways to keep your mind off your worries.

This began to drive a lot of demand for our products, and we knew that a lot of our customers were at home with a bit more time on their hands and that some of the older ones especially might be feeling a bit anxious. We wanted to keep everyone's hands moving, using up all that nervous energy, to keep people really engaged, feeling a bit of community and positivity. People seemed to want and need something to focus on that wasn't the rolling news.

A lot of our customers were in the States, where things had become a lot more febrile a lot more quickly. Trump was still president at the time, there was an election on the horizon, and it felt like there were even more people over there who were looking to escape non-stop controversy. So we made it an informal rule that we would not talk about the pandemic. We wanted to create a haven, a safe space where people could tune in and know that those outside anxieties would not interrupt them for however long they were watching.

I should say that this policy was not just a cold-hearted business decision – I had re-discovered for myself the incredible therapeutic qualities of crafting during those first few months of the pandemic. Obviously, crafting is my business, but this was a period when it felt very far from being a busman's holiday to be working with my hands myself.

Like almost everyone, we used to watch that government briefing every night. The statistics were so grim, and the tone so bleak, you just used to wait for that briefing all day with a sense of dread. Then, after a couple of weeks, I was like, 'There's got to be more to life than waiting for this briefing.' So instead of watching TV on a night, waiting for that briefing, I looked up online how to crochet a rainbow to hang in the window. I ordered some yarn and a crochet hook – I hadn't crocheted since my grandma taught me when I was six – and followed this tutorial on how to crochet the rainbow. It took me a couple of hours that first night, so the next night I did another one for my in-laws. Then the next night I did one for my mam and dad to put in their window. After a while, I could do one of these rainbows in half an hour. It was my thing, my switch-off.

I was reminded why craft is so good for us. All the research that has been done around this shows that it's because it gives you something to do with your hands and it keeps your mind occupied, but not too much. We were tuning into those press conferences, knowing that we didn't have a clue what was going to happen next. But with craft, after you've done a couple of pairs of socks or crochet rainbows, or whatever, you think, 'There's certainty. Follow the pattern, and you'll have done it.' And there's that real sense of achievement, the positive endorphins that are released – you feel good!

There are a lot of forums online, full of people who are making things and sharing pictures of what they've made, and all their friends are telling them how awesome it is, and then, on top of that, you're often gifting people things. I ended up working with the charity Mind, teaching online classes, because I could see how good it was for mental health because of how good it had been for my own.

The beautiful thing about consciously setting this

tone and posting the broadcasts on our social media channels was that we could see a lot of the viewers starting to connect and make friends with each other – and us! We started to do the shows daily, posting them on YouTube and Facebook each time so that our community could get together and feel that safe space in a regular way.

Then, as global quarantines kicked in, I couldn't go over to America to film like I used to do. The shopping channels in the US – and Germany not long after – made the decision that the only staff they were now going to have onsite were the main presenters and key crew. No more guests in the studios, even the ones who lived right there in the same state. They wanted to keep the presenters safe, isolated, so that they could keep regular broadcasts going for as long as possible. The American channels started saying, 'Well, we'll take your Skype feed in on an iPhone.'

So, with a lot of their other guests, their husbands would be stood in the kitchen with an iPhone while they were showing you their products and doing their utmost to sell their stock, with the kitchen table and perhaps a couple of kids in shot. But we had this whole amazing studio set up for Crafter's TV so we used that studio to broadcast the output to the various shopping channels. And because it looks so professional, and we were so well geared up to do it, all the channels started taking more from us, giving us more slots, especially in the UK, because we were already set up to do the output. So we were able to keep business continuity with the shopping channels we supplied just by working in a very different way, plus we ramped up the shows we were doing through Crafter's TV to our own audience. Almost before we knew it, we were doing all the support and educational shows we had always done, plus we started doing shows once or twice a week where we would essentially be like the shopping channel and sell off the old stock we had in the warehouse. We were turning our stock into cash and creating a new revenue stream to support the business through this rocky period.

Before the pandemic, the studio was literally the shed in the corner of the car park, and we'd put some soundproofing and a few cameras in it. And then, over the first six months of the pandemic, it took off so much that we ended up building a second studio in the shed, spending thousands on equipment, and making it even more high-tech.

Then, by the winter lockdown – and this was a difficult decision for me – we decided to permanently close our flagship store by our head office, take out all the fittings and convert the 5,000-square-foot shop space into two brand-new state-of-the-art studios. At the time, it was one of those calls that is so hard to make, because we had fifteen staff in that shop. We were able to find some of them jobs within other areas of the business, but some of them didn't want other jobs, they wanted to work in a craft shop. So it was really hard that we had to lose some staff – although, in the end, in the new year, we actually gained more staff because we recruited so many to work on this new, exciting Crafter's TV venture.

The only thing I found disappointing about this huge creative burst the lockdown provided was that it wasn't sustainable – for me more than for the business. When the kids went back to school I felt a huge change in myself almost immediately. At first, I couldn't understand why I felt differently. All of a sudden, I had gone from this person who was getting up at stupid o'clock every day – willingly – and going for a run, and now I couldn't drag my sorry ass out of bed in time to get the kids into school. It was only later – last year when I left *Strictly* – that Deborah Meaden explained it to me. She pointed out that when there is that huge surge of adrenaline during enormous life events, such as that first lockdown or taking part in *Strictly*, you can fire on all cylinders, for weeks or months if you need to. But when you stop needing the adrenaline, you hit the most enormous slump. And I really, really did – both times. That life was only sustainable for so long. I want to be the person who wants to get up at five o'clock every morning, not the one who can only do it when there is a major situation playing out, but I don't know if I ever will be. I was just glad I had Deborah to share her pearls of wisdom with me about what I was going through physically.

I will cherish the fact that I learned I could do it at all, though. I found reserves of resilience during the pandemic that I never imagined I had. But the best thing about it was one of the most unexpected: I put my boys to bed myself every single night for a year. And that was something I had never been able to do in my life.

In the year since, things ramped up significantly, especially with *Strictly* of course, but even before that I was having to go to America once a month, and it was for four days each time. In many ways, I loved it – it was my dream career, my own business and, of course, a little breather from two pre-schoolers is often welcome when you're in those early years. But the experience of being there for every single bedtime during that year was life-changing for me. I absolutely loved it, and so did they.

The fact that we were so well prepared to broadcast in the States from our own premises was one of the most significant factors in us surviving the pandemic the way we did. And it was also the thing that enabled me to take on my next big challenge. Because I could keep broadcasting on HSN from my home town, when they decided that they would not be having guests in the studio until at least January 2022 I no longer needed to take my once-monthly trips to Florida to make my appearances. Which in turn meant that I was able to say yes to my biggest challenge yet: *Strictly Come Dancing*.

Chapter 10

Leave it on the Dance Floor

———

I don't think it is a huge secret that it was a life-long dream of mine to take part in *Strictly Come Dancing*. But I had no idea that, if I actually got to do it, the experience would exceed even my *very* high expectations.

First, I had to get myself asked to take part, which was a mission in itself – even for someone as used to selling themselves as I am. Almost as soon as I got the job at *Dragons' Den*, I made sure that every single person I chatted to in 'TV Land' understood my passion for *Strictly Come Dancing*. And when I hired an agent, I made sure that she in turn was telling everyone who mattered.

Every year there are clients of the TV agency that represents me who will be asked to do the show, and I never quite understood how it worked, whether the agents put clients forward or if the BBC scouted around for people. But I made sure I covered all eventualities, using any opportunity to tell anybody senior at the BBC – albeit slightly tongue-in-cheek – what my dream was. For example, when I was asked to go on the celebrity edition of another BBC quiz show, I politely declined because I didn't think it was right for me, but I made sure I ended my message by adding at the bottom of the email, 'I wish you were the commissioner for the other fun shows . . . like the dancing one, for example . . .'

For years, I put the earworm in with enough people in the industry, but I never knew if it was doing any good, or if I would even be in a position to accept if anyone did show any interest in letting me on the show. For most contestants, *Strictly Come Dancing* is a job that gives them a chance to reach new audiences and develop a career in TV even further. But for me, my main job at Crafter's Companion already takes up most of my time, and it's nothing to do with TV. On top of that, the cost to the business of me being essentially 'missing in action' for several months was in the hundreds of thousands – way more than the fee the BBC offers any of the contestants to do the show. But it was my passion – it had always been my passion, ever since seeing Jill Halfpenny doing the North-East proud by knocking it out of the park with her iconic jive.

The Davieses taking time off is not something that the company is very used to. To be honest, it's very rare that Simon and I take any time off. We have short holidays and days out with the kids, but we have never taken any more than a week off work, certainly never considered anything like sabbaticals or indulged in any time-consuming side projects. Despite this, over the years I have carried a massive amount of guilt at the sacrifices others have made so that I could get the company up to the level it is, while being a good mam. What I had never done was take time out to do something simply *for me*.

So when the text came from my agent I couldn't believe my luck. I was halfway through filming the last series of *Dragons' Den* when she texted me to say that I should call her on my lunch break. So I did, and all she said was 'I've had that call . . .'

'What call?' I replied.

'*That* call . . .'

'Oh my god!' My heart was pounding. But my agent said, 'I think we should wait and do it next year – I don't think you'd get the full experience, because it's still going to be operating under Covid guidelines. You're not going to be going to Blackpool, there isn't going to be the usual audience, you might not be able to really live it to the full . . .'

'I don't care,' I replied straight away. 'I'm not bothered about an audience. I'm not bothered about

Blackpool. I can do it this year because I'm not going to be travelling to America. This is my time. I've earned it.'

And I really think I had. I never had the full university experience, staying out too late and skipping lectures, or going travelling all over the world first. I worked all hours for my degree while setting up Crafter's Companion, and I have worked non-stop since then. I had done nearly twenty years of hard graft in corporate life, with all the travel, long hours and compromises that entails. I knew the business might suffer as a result of me not being able to give it my all for a few months. I would *have* to take a substantial amount of time off. But this chance to do *Strictly* was coming along the one year I was not bound by constant flights to the US. Truly, it was a once-in-a-lifetime opportunity to live my dream and follow my passion – just for the sake of it.

As with *Dragons' Den*, I had a Zoom call with the production team so they could try and understand why I wanted to do the show and if I really and truly understood what it would entail – had I grasped how physically demanding it would be? Or how huge the time commitment was?

The answer to all of the questions was yes. And as for me wanting to do it, it was the biggest yes of all. They took quite some convincing that I really did just want to do the show for the sake of it! I had absolutely no bloody clue how to dance. After all, it wasn't going to give me a leg-up in my career and, if anything, I was apprehensive about becoming any more well known. Those were quite often the other contestants' key drivers to take part!

But I had wanted to access this part of myself for so long. A physical, creative, dynamic self that the life I had led so far simply hadn't had space for before. Now, it wasn't as if the life I had been leading hadn't been a happy one – quite the opposite! – but it had been a busy one. And now there was this window of post-pandemic time where I could make it work . . .

I guess that is why people enjoyed watching me and Aljaž Škorjanec dancing together for as long as they did: they could see that I just enjoyed the dancing for its own sake. And for any of you who are still left wondering – yes, it was everything I had hoped it would be. And so much more.

Since I left the show, I have said to people that it was a life-changing experience, and then they want to understand how. Surely it was just dancing, and not even to the final? I suppose that's what I thought at first as well. But the change it has inspired in me has been huge. I went into it with that same old attitude that I first developed at university: the harder I work, the better the results. It was the case with exams, and then with my business – with life! And I thought that *Strictly* would be the same, but with dance steps – that it would just be down to the hours I put in in the training room, that it was somehow like athletics, that I could get myself there with graft and determination.

Well, how wrong I was, and how much I learned. Let's not pretend it wasn't hard work, though. There were huge physical demands on me. And before the live shows had even started, I realized that the pressure on my home and business life really was going to be more intense than even I had prepared for.

From the minute I met Aljaž up by the Angel of the North for that first introductory show, I immediately became swept up in the excitement of the *Strictly* experience. I had had no idea that I would be partnered with him until I saw him that day with the cameras rolling but, as ever, I had hardly kept quiet about the fact that I would like to be. Someone asked me if I was 'putting it out into the universe' that I'd like him as a partner.

'Sure,' I said, 'if "putting it out into the universe" is simply telling any producer who'll listen that I think I'd like to work with him.' Ever since he joined the show, I'd imagined I would click with Aljaž, and when I knew I was going to be taking part I only became more convinced. Having shared the experience with him, I can't even imagine what it would be like to go through it with someone who you didn't get on so well with.

From the very next day, when we started training for

the first live show, I was dancing for several hours a day, every day, and totally committed to training. After all, the hard work would pay off, wouldn't it? Then I was coming home on a night and talking about the dancing and showing Simon the videos of how we'd got on that day. Next, I was inviting Aljaž home to come and have tea with us so we could all talk about the dancing. Later in the evening, I'd be spending ages on social media, updating Instagram, and so on.

Meanwhile, Simon was living like a single parent. On top of his day job as CEO of the company, he was also having to take on all the stuff that I usually manage in the business: overseeing the staff who report in to me, going to all the meetings I usually go to. And he was having to do more with the kids. Even when I wasn't down in London, I was going out at six o'clock in the morning, so he was still getting the boys up, dressed, out to school, doing football training, on to swimming lessons ... absolutely everything. And it wasn't just Simon, our whole family chipped in – our parents, my sister – it literally took an army to keep the show on the road in my semi-absence.

Then, one Friday night, the weekend between me being introduced to Aljaž and that first live show, I caught myself. We had a big meeting with the US at half past seven, so I had to get the kids to bed first, then I went and sat with my feet in a bucket of iced water during a board meeting from half past seven to eleven o'clock. Right up until moments before we logged on to the meeting, I'd been chewing Simon's ear off about the show, on this massive endorphin high from all the dancing, then I confessed to him that I hadn't actually had time to do the prep work for the meeting. In admitting that, I was letting slip that I had basically rendered three or four hours of work time he was putting in useless, as the team would now have to waste time on the call explaining everything I should have prepped for in the pre-reading . . .

Just as I said it, I realized that he was starting to get a bit ratty with the kids, which is something he *never* does. And it hit me. He wasn't getting ratty with them – even if they were scamping around when we needed them in bed in time for the meeting. He was feeling ratty with me. Because I hadn't been at home all day, I'd been out strutting around with some dancer guy, then I'd come home, put my feet in an ice bucket, faffed around on my phone for a couple of hours, admitted I wasn't prepared for what I needed to do – oh, and I'd had the audacity to ask for a bit of emotional support on top (as I had quickly learned that the whole experience was an emotional roller coaster from the first week!).

No wonder the guy was ratty. Even when he finally had the chance to get his head on the pillow at night, I wasn't thinking to ask how *he* was, I'd only been firing questions about the business, what I'd missed, what I felt I 'needed' to know. Boundaries were being trampled all over the shop.

Later that evening, I realized that my behaviour, if not my enthusiasm for trying to do it all, needed to be reined in a little if we were all going to get to Christmas without tearing each other's hair out. I had a few words with myself and, after that, everything felt a little calmer. In truth, that night was the wake-up call I needed. I decided, 'Right, I'm just going to leave him to run the business for a bit. I'm going to do the bits that are needed, like my crafting TV shows, but I have to stop spending our family time trying to micromanage what everyone else is up to while I'm not in the office.'

I reminded myself of my own golden rule: *be present.* And after that, I was.

A week later came the first live show, when Aljaž and I did our first dance. And therein was the next of my enormous learning experiences. We were doing the cha-cha-cha, our *Dragons' Den*-themed routine to 'The Boss' by Diana Ross. When we finished, I was thrilled with how it had gone. I had worked so hard on every single step. And I nailed it! The Cuban breaks and the lock-steps, the New Yorkers – I knew I had absolutely got the technique down and had delivered them just right.

But when the judges' comments – and then the

scores – came in, they told a different story. They said that I hadn't given it my all. What?! I couldn't have trained any harder, or put any more work in. I didn't understand it. And as the rest of the competitors' scores came in, my heart only sank further. We had danced fifth out of everyone, and when I was at the bottom immediately I assumed that, as ten further dancers came in, *some* of them would score below me. But no one did, not a single couple. The leaderboard just kept stretching upwards and upwards above me, name upon name piling up above ours as we stayed stubbornly at the bottom. 'Fair enough, it's only week one,' I tried to tell myself. But I was devastated.

Over the course of the evening, I got more and more distraught about it. But I was absolutely determined not to show it, because I had learned over the years that that was no path to success. In business, there's no space for being vulnerable; you have to put up a sort of armour when you're in a corporate environment. Even if I am the least 'put-on-a-front'-type businessperson out there, I still know that projecting the image of a strong, powerful businesswoman – particularly if I'm not feeling it inside – is the way to do it. Given that I now have twenty years of putting on that armour, I thought I was pretty damn good at it.

All evening, Aljaž kept saying to me, 'Are you all right?' and I kept replying with variations on 'Yeah, I'm fine.'

'I'm fine, it was only the first time.'

'I'm okay with it.'

'Yeah, I'm great.'

And so on.

But it was just a coping mechanism to keep saying that I was not bothered. Of course I was. And I had severely underestimated Aljaž – and his innate ability to see through that armour and see how I was really feeling. At one point he just looked me in the eye, quite emotional, and said, 'It really broke my heart tonight, seeing how upset you were.'

I thought he had had no idea! I had assumed I had fooled everyone, so how come he had seen past the armour? But he had, and that's because he's a dancer – they aren't just listening to what you're saying, they are also experts in reading your body language. And that is when I realized that I really *was* deep in the *Strictly* experience. I was in a world where I was playing by different rules than the ones I'd been playing by in the rest of my career. Hard work alone was no longer going to cut it. This time, I had to make the emotional connection to dancing, and I knew that my body might give me away even if my face didn't.

The next day, I watched our dance back and the penny finally dropped. I could see that everybody else had gone out there and left their heart on the dance floor, putting everything into their performance emotionally. No reservations, no anxieties, just pure, open-hearted performance. And I hadn't. Yes, I'd nailed the steps, but I had also kept that damn armour up. And it showed. As I watched all the other performances, it slowly dawned on me – what I had thought was going to be about acting, learning to pretend, was actually about letting myself go there – feeling the dance, becoming absolutely present in it. And I had never done that. Yet another huge wake-up call for me.

Thankfully, on that first weekend there was no elimination, or I would have been a goner straight away. Now, I had a week to learn a foxtrot, as well as completely revise my approach to performance. Mercifully, I had Aljaž by my side.

Quite quickly, we got ourselves into a little bit of a weekly routine that allowed me to get as much practice in as possible while also doing as many school pick-ups as I could and not entirely deserting my role at Crafter's Companion. It was a squeeze, but it just about worked for us. I found us a little dance studio only seven miles from my house, a lovely little family-run business, and they even trusted me enough to give me my own set of keys so we could let ourselves in first thing.

We'd meet there at six o'clock every morning for the first half of the week, and Aljaž would go and make us some coffee while I went round turning all the lights on, including the glitter ball over the centre of the dance floor. It was a really traditional space, a proper dancing school with a lovely ballroom floor exactly the same size as the one used at the *Strictly* studio. My dad even used to dance there back in the day.

They had amended their own class timetable to give us as much time to rehearse as possible. We'd arrive there in the weeks when late summer turned into autumn and the mornings started to get darker and darker, and sometimes it felt like we were the only people in the world who were up and about. It seemed a million miles away from the noise and sparkles of the *Strictly* studio; it was a safe place where I could really focus on learning the dance steps and trying to harness that bit of me that the judges and the public would need to see if I was going to stay in the competition.

Perhaps 'harness' is the wrong word, as what was required of me was more of a letting-go. And it took some persuading. Aljaž has the highest level of emotional intelligence of anybody I've ever come across. Anybody. And bear in mind, I train in emotional intelligence, I coach my staff in emotional intelligence, so I'm very clued into it. But he is off the chart. He was able to gradually persuade, cajole and explain to me that just trying harder wasn't going to be enough on the dance floor. I had to relax into the performance too.

I like learning. I have always been one to take courses and improve gaps in my knowledge. I enjoy going on business seminars where you learn about business techniques, and I enjoy things like leadership coaching where the approach is more about psychology. But what I really loved about learning with Aljaž was that he's such a great teacher and he's totally passionate about his subject too.

There were several ways in which this manifested itself, and each one was something I had never encountered in the business world. The first was that uncanny ability to read body language. When you're dancing together, you're not always looking at each other eye to eye, so the professional dancers are all very good at reading body language. To be at that level you have got to be able to read your partner's body, even if you can't always see it, and Aljaž was exceptional. That week after our cha-cha-cha, he explained, 'I can feel everything without you saying a word to me,' and despite that sounding absolutely baffling, he was right. He knew exactly when I had gone wrong on a step, even if he was looking straight over my shoulder with no hope of seeing my feet. He could do it because he could feel my body tense up. I would say, 'Oh damn it, when we did the New Yorkers, I messed up the hip,' and he would say calmly, 'I know, I felt your shoulders go because you were disappointed with yourself.' It really was incredible how he can read the body from holding you when you dance, and it meant that I learned quite quickly that I couldn't blag it with him or pretend when things weren't quite right.

And this was on top of the fact that I had already learned that I couldn't bluff my emotions – he had already proved that he could see right through that. And then there was the way he taught me the different types of dance. Each time he introduced new types of steps, we worked on them in certain ways that sort of hoodwinked me into not realizing what I had learned. He would push me into doing a move that was artificial, quite over the top, in order to build up my muscle memory, to take away my fear of doing the step itself, then a couple of days later he'd pull it back a little, to the *actual* step. And there was the way we learned the dances, doing the feet first, not worrying about what dancers call 'the frame' (I quickly realized it was 'the arm bit'). We'd add the frame in later, once I felt confident with the feet. So instead of doing the first few seconds of the dance hundreds of times, then the next few seconds, and so on, it was more a gradual process of layering on the techniques, building up my confidence and revealing what I had really learned towards the second half of the week.

He never said to me, 'This is what we're learning today,' but chatted around it, keeping me distracted from the idea of 'doing it right' and focused on the idea of connecting with the dance as a whole. And my god did it work – one week I found out that Emma Thompson – Dame Emma Thompson! – had taken him to one side and said, 'How did you teach Sara that?

How, in four days, have you taught an absolute beginner how to do that? That's just magical.' And it was – but the most magical bit of all was that I wasn't even aware that that's what he'd been doing, for weeks. I guess that is how he is one of the best in the world at what he does, both the dancing and the teaching.

Then there was the final layer of the Aljaž magic: the fact that he also possessed the specific skill of being able to be a happily married man, in a totally secure relationship, while also spending hours at a time, at all hours, with someone else, teaching them to access their emotions in a way that makes not just *them* feel safe but *their entire family* too. For someone who has worked on their boundaries as much as I have, it was like watching a masterclass in knowing oneself and being secure in where those boundaries lay.

I once asked them at dinner how his wife, Janette, copes with the fact that every year she's got to give her husband up for three or four months while another woman spends half the day with her arms wrapped around him and the other half leaning on him emotionally. She simply explained that she had been a pro on the show for eight years too, so she had done exactly the same thing, with a male partner, on many occasions. Later, once we had got to know each other, Janette confirmed this. They simply understand that *Strictly* is a work environment for them, in perhaps the same way that some of the staff at Crafter's Companion can't understand how Simon and I can live and work together.

Aljaž and I would stay in our little dance-school bubble for the first half of the week, with him over time being integrated into the Davies family more and more. At first he was in the back seat during school pick-up, then he was coming along to swimming lessons before having dinner with us and reading the boys their bedtime stories. This meant that they very soon went from seeing *Strictly* as a mythical enterprise that took their mammy away from home to something that meant Aljaž, their cool new uncle, was coming to football practice. I think he started off doing those things to reassure them, to get the whole family onside, but then, in time, it seemed to become something he enjoyed for its own sake.

We'd usually break out of the North-East bubble by Wednesday night, when I would usually stay to put the boys to bed, and once they were asleep creep back out of their bedroom, load up the car and be driven down to London, ready to do things like *It Takes Two* on the Thursday. I would get down to the city by about one o'clock in the morning, but as I had slept in the back of the car, and the dance studio we rehearsed in down there didn't open until eight in the morning, I always had what felt like an enormous lie-in!

Fridays were studio days: the chance to see your costume for the first time and to rehearse on the famous dance floor with the band, both of which are major parts of the *Strictly* experience. The team has a manne-quin made up to each of the contestants' and the professionals' measurements and an outside company makes up a base costume for each week's dance. It arrives at the studio for Friday, you try it on and then they set about '*Strictly*-fying' it. They add slits into the fabric, trim the hem if it's too long, add an overskirt to give more movement, and start adding stones and sequins. So very, very many stones and sequins. The fact that they can't really get going with these details until we try them on on a Friday is why it always seems to be going so close to the wire on a Saturday – because that's what's really happening. A good 90 per cent of what you would remember of the costume is put together in that last thirty-six hours, sewing machines, glue guns and scissors going nineteen to the dozen.

It would be a little bit sneaky not to admit to how much was going on *under* the dresses, though . . . When I first met the costume team on a video call, I told them that I was really conscious of my wobbly tummy but that I also didn't want to look like I was embar-rassed by myself, and they immediately reassured me: 'Don't worry – we can do all sorts of things to help you with that. We'll just build more hemlines under the bust, put ruching in across the tummy, all kinds of tricks.' Plus, there were corsets, Spanx . . . in fact, more often than not a corset *and* Spanx. That first week, when Craig Revel Horwood's comment about my cha-cha-cha was that I would 'have to move my hips a bit more', what I wanted to say was 'Well, you try moving your hips while pulled into a corset, covered with a pair of Spanx and with another pair of additional support pants sewn into your dress for good measure!' but I didn't – I just smiled a great big smile at him and pretended everything was all right!

To start with, that was my choice, because I was so conscious of my tummy. I wasn't ashamed of my body as such – I've always been quite happy to embrace the fact that I had a bit of a mum tum. I just didn't want to look like I was going wiggling it all over the dance floor. I'm more of the opinion of, if you haven't got it, maybe don't go flaunting it anyway. But it's a fine balance between not looking ashamed of yourself and flaunting your tummy without a care in the world. Mercifully, the *Strictly* team have seen a lot of body types pass through their doors and a lot of physical transformations, so nothing I threw at them seemed to faze them.

Even if the gem-glue was sometimes still drying on my dress when we hit the dance floor, I never felt less than a million dollars when I did. By the time Aljaž and I returned with our foxtrot to 'Dream a Little Dream' for week two – the first week there was an elimination – I had come to realize that our performance was the culmination of so many exceptionally talented people's skills and dedication and I was determined not to let anyone down. I now saw that the only thing worse than ending up looking a fool would be to look like someone trying to *avoid* looking a fool. I had to throw myself into the moment and ride the wave of all their communal efforts and goodwill.

And, what do you know – it worked! Top of the leaderboard! We got such great comments, and the atmosphere in the room was incredible. Most special of all was that Simon was in the audience that night to experience the magical moment with me. The dance, and then the response, was the biggest buzz I had had since those very first days live on shopping TV fifteen years before. This time, I had Aljaž there with me, and I was so delighted not to have let all his patience and wisdom come to nothing. I'd lost myself in the dance, and it had paid off in buckets.

Once we were away from the cameras, Aljaž even shed a few tears at how proud and excited he was that I had made that emotional connection with the dance. I had felt that in his body language while we were on the dance floor, and then when we were receiving the judges' comments, but moments later it was an extraordinarily humbling experience to see that even after years of doing this – and doing it at a whole different level – the professionals still care *this much* about each and every dance. It just made me even more determined to try even harder to do his hard work justice.

We headed back up to the North-East after the show, back to our little dance studio on the Monday morning, and his suggestion for the next week's dance for movie week was *Shrek*. I think a lot of viewers thought I must have been livid at this suggestion, what with the bile-green tights and fake bobbly nose, but I wasn't at all. In fact, my first instinct was to check that I would only be doing it 'As long as I can be big green Princess Fiona and not the pretty one.' Because as much as I had enjoyed my foxtrot, it was a ballroom dance, not a Latin one, and this week we were doing a samba. The big difference between the ballroom and the Latin dances is that with the ballroom ones you can look elegant, composed and, above all, you can stay in the arms of your partner. With the Latin dances, you really have to sell yourself – and often you have to do half of that across the room from your partner – doing your own, dazzling thing.

The trouble with this kind of dance is that it's basic-ally a sort of sanctioned showing-off. I went back to feeling like a bit of a tit about it. You have to be so content to go 'Woooohoooo, look at me!' in the Latin dances, which I naturally am not inclined to do. Sure, I might be very confident doing a live crafting session broadcast to millions of homes across America – I barely break a sweat then, when the odd mistake makes me look human and might even create sales. But there's no space for that on the dance floor. Making a messy card with charm is not quite in the same ballpark as shaking my hips to half the UK's Saturday-night viewers while covered in glitter.

So I leapt at the chance to be green Princess Fiona, because it meant I could hide behind a character. No one would think I was trying to be the sexiest mam in town. There could be no 'Who *does* she think she is?' if the answer was . . . Princess Fiona. What did they think I'd be thinking? 'Hey, fellas, look at me, I'm painted green and I've got a fat suit on'? That outfit required a silly, self-deprecating British type of humour that I knew I could do well, so I didn't feel too self-conscious. And, once again, the judges and the audience at home loved it. They could not believe we had pulled off those daft costumes, and I am not sure we could either!

As the weeks rolled by, with Aljaž's careful tuition and with me spending more time with the cast and crew each week, I started to see that there is nothing so wrong with a bit of showing-off. Why bother going to all that effort to get on the show, why put in all of those hours of training, why revel in every sparkle of those incredible costumes if you're then going to get on the dance floor and have an attack of 'Don't look at me, I'm shy'?

By week four, when we were due to do the tango, I had reconciled myself to the fact that *Strictly Come Dancing is all about* showing-off, and that's fine. No one thinks you're an idiot for showing off when you are literally on a dance floor with a spotlight on you, a mobile-camera operator dancing around you to catch your every move. Just as people *wanted* to learn when they were watching me fold my envelopes or sew a patchwork cushion cover, when they have had a bit of a crappy week and finally made it to Saturday and settled down with a glass of wine for the evening, they *want* to be dazzled. Who wants to see someone with their armour up when they've had their own armour up all week? Let the sequins fly!

When we came down to London that week, I saw the base dress that had been made for me to tango in and was given the chance to try it on. It was a gorgeous deep purple but had a very dropped hem, basically below my stomach. When I put it on, the head of wardrobe immediately said to me, 'Look, I know you're not going to be happy about where the hem is, so I can move it – we haven't had it stitched on so we can move it up straight away if you want us to.'

I didn't say anything, just looked at myself in the dress.

'A tango dress *would* look like this,' she carried on, 'but I know you're not comfortable.'

She pinned it where it could be if they changed it from the traditional silhouette to something more discreet for me and my tum.

'I think your body shape has changed so much in the last five weeks that you'll look really good in it,' she continued, 'but I don't want you going out there feeling uncomfortable, because then you won't do your best dance.'

And almost before I had the chance to stop myself, I heard my own voice saying, 'If *you* think I look all right in it, I'm going to try it.' So I did. And I was so proud of myself for wearing that dropped hem. Yes, my tummy is bigger than I would want it to be, but at least I didn't let it stop me from doing the dance properly. And it didn't just not stop me from doing the dance properly, it helped me to absolutely nail it. Once again, the gradual shedding of my inhibitions paid off, and we were through to week five. By now, I was massively emotionally invested in the show and I was having the time of my life.

The next week it was the rumba, and that's the one where you have to really move your hips. Aljaž and I were in our little routine now, working hard for the first half of the week, then back in wardrobe by Friday. This time I just turned up and announced straight away, 'I'm not wearing the corset this week. I'm not doing it, because I'm not going to restrict my hip movement.' That week we were dancing to Shania Twain's 'You're Still the One' and the team were suggesting a choice between an off-the-peg wrap dress that they would '*Strictly*-fy' or a more regular dress that would be slightly tighter across my stomach. So I chose the wrap dress, because I knew that it would meet under the bust, flowing more loosely across my middle and giving me that little bit more confidence if I was dancing without the corset. It worked – I moved my hips with confident fluidity and, bingo, we were through again! I was so thrilled with myself.

Learning not to rely on a corset was a massive step for me, but while my confidence was surging, the physical impact of all the dancing was really starting to take its toll on me in all sorts of other ways. What I had not appreciated before we started was that every single dance would be physically demanding on me in a totally different way. The Argentine tango took it out of my quads because of all the lunges – so painful! The foxtrot was all in my calves, driving through my standing leg again and again. After the samba, my hips were exhausted, and with some of the other ballroom styles it was the balls of my feet that took the pressure. I was spending increasing amounts of time in physio, massage, getting my legs taped up, sitting with my feet in more buckets of ice, stretching at all hours. Yet the ailments would kind of disappear as quickly as they came, because you'd be on to working different muscles in your body as the dances changed each week.

As the weeks passed, more people started to comment on whether I was losing weight, and the truth is I didn't lose a single pound on the scales. But I could tell that my body shape was changing – by the time I left the show I was wearing dresses I hadn't for ten years, partly because they hadn't fitted properly, and partly because I hadn't had the confidence before.

Weight loss felt even less important than ever, though. The real joy was in feeling my fitness levels rise and my stamina increasing as we practised more and more hours each week. The more I wanted to dance, the stronger I got, and the more I found I could dance. Before, the driving factor in me wanting to lose weight had been to do with health reasons: wanting to be in good shape to get pregnant, needing to keep my BMI down, and so on. Now, I felt myself appreciate my body more than ever because it was letting me dance more than ever. Even with the aching thighs, calves and hips, every step was a joy.

No matter how much I loved the dancing, I cannot lie and pretend that the tiredness did not start to get to me. Some weeks, especially towards the end, the hours I was working were getting quite extreme. I was getting a few hours' sleep in the back of the car up and down the motorway, snatching a couple more after appearing on TV shows at all hours and then the odd Sunday nap after the live show between kids' birthday parties and football matches.

I have definitely always been able to push myself further than most people are prepared to. This time, I found myself thinking, 'Well, it's not that I can't phys- ically do it. Yes, I'm hurting, but that's just because it's new. I'm not going to be doing this for ever, so try to see past the pain, the tiredness, and enjoy every minute.'

It reminded me of when I was pregnant, sitting in antenatal classes thinking, 'Yup, this sounds really painful. But there must be an element of mind over matter here. It is pain that's going to end. It's pain that's worth it. So you've got to breathe your way through it and know that it's going to come to an end.' My children's births were not quite that simple, but you get the sentiment. I can often find ways to push myself past tiredness and pain if I think the goal is worth it.

As pressure mounted up from work, TV appearances, family commitments and beyond, I found myself returning to my old advice to be present whenever I could. Just as I used to work on the flight back from the States so I could devote myself fully to mam-time when I got back, I found myself having to mentally compartmentalize in a similar way. I could have lost myself in panicking about my inbox if I had looked at my emails while we were having a water break sitting at the side of the dance floor. Or I could have spent board meetings running over steps in my head. But I had to slam those mental doors shut. For me to learn the dances properly, I had to be one hundred per cent focused on the dance. I made sure never to schedule any work calls until after we had got our six or seven hours of practice in, because if I had taken even one that had distracted me, it would have wasted the next two hours of dancing, as my mind would have been elsewhere. And then, the minute the dance practice was over, I was trying to fit the whole of the rest of my life into a day that was now six or seven hours shorter. More often than not, I'd work on an evening: do the school pick-up, then, once I had got the kids to bed, I'd be catching up on emails, taking calls and meetings with teams in China or the US – and working on this book! My staff adjusted their schedules to do some work meetings late on an evening, I would do TV shows through the night to the US and then it was back up and raring to go all over again by six o'clock the next morning.

The only thing that really and truly fell by the way-side was self-care. I have never been great at that anyway, but by November it was really stripped to essentials only. I would have the massage lady come round, and she would always want to do something a bit relaxing, but I was never into it.

'I haven't got time! You want to give me a nice back massage to help me wind down because you think I'm stressed, but the only thing stressing me out is that I haven't got an hour in my day to give you! I need you to pummel my legs for forty-five minutes and then go to the balls of my feet for fifteen. And yes, I *know* it's going to be painful.'

'Sometimes you just need to relax,' she'd implore. 'And more than that, it'll probably help you a bit more than just being pummelled.' But I'd never let her. Even when I got down to London and had the luxury of a hotel room to myself, with no kids to wake me up, I would go out and talk dancing with Aljaž or anyone from the show who was around. Why would I lie in a bath and watch TV when I could be inhaling every moment of my *Strictly* time?

Just a week later I felt entirely vindicated in my choices because, just as I had started to think it might all go on for ever, my *Strictly* journey came to what felt like an abrupt end. I loved the Argentine tango we did that week, and I loved the whole 'look'. But the competition was getting so good and, once all the contestants had danced, Aljaž and I were left in the middle of the leaderboard, which is always the most dangerous place to be. People at home assume you're safe as you're not at the bottom, and the window of time they have to vote in is so small that if they're not actively worried about you going, they might not put in that vote for you.

I made no secret about how sad I was to end my journey that night, and even now I don't quite feel that it was my time to go. But it wasn't a bad time. I certainly exceeded a lot of people's expectations, including my own. It might have left a sour taste if I had gone out on a week when I really was at the bottom of the leaderboard. I would have felt so negative if it had been a week when the judges hadn't loved our routine, like the week we did the Couple's Choice with a Mother of Dragon's-style routine, which Aljaž had thought was sensational but no one else seemed that fussed by.

What else could I have done? I put in the work, I truly threw myself at living the dance, and I was right to have let myself enjoy every single second of it. It's a compliment that people thought I was too safe to vote for – I really was blown away by the level of support we had week after week, from the general public and from all the campaigns and banners when we were up at home in the North-East.

But none of this means that I didn't need to do a bit of good old-fashioned wallowing that first week I was out. I went out for dinner with Aljaž, had too much wine and way too many tears once or twice, but when the clouds parted I realized how much I had to return to.

My tears dry, I saw that everything was still there, waiting for me. My incredible family, who have been behind me in everything I've done, since day one. And my career and my business. All those choices along the way had stood me in good stead. My family had sacrificed so much for me to be able to be on the show, and I wanted to repay them in full, with weeks of Christmas fun and love. As the year drew to an end and I recognized the good friendships I had made, the wonderful experiences I had had and the enormous amount I had learned about myself, I saw with clearer and clearer eyes not what I no longer had but how much I had gained.

Epilogue

I f there was one key lesson that I learned from last year's experience on *Strictly Come Dancing*, it was that being vulnerable in front of others is no bad thing, and in a lot of cases it might even be quite powerful. After all, the only certain way to look weak is to look embarrassed by what you're doing.

Perhaps you think that ending a powerful business memoir by praising the value of vulnerability is not the done thing. I might have thought the same a few years ago. But what I hope you have taken from hearing my story is that staying honest about who you are is one of the most important attributes you can have. And coming from a completely ordinary family is another.

As I said at the beginning of this book, many business-people I meet – especially women – and people who aren't in business themselves assume that I must have had some sort of leg-up along the way. Now you can see that there was no one skeleton key that unlocked my career. I simply made the most of each choice as it came along and worked as hard as I could in between those choices.

I have been very honest with you here, and I do hope you haven't just felt that I've been chewing your ear off about sequins and purchase order numbers for the hell of it. Because there has been a method to my madness: I truly believe that if I show you my mistakes, my low points and my learning moments, you can see how I got to where I am.

I hope that you can see how the ability to be present has helped me to focus when I really needed to, and to relax when I needed that too. I hope that you have learned how important it is to get the details down on paper when success – no matter how exciting! – makes its first appearance. And I hope you have taken on board the power of separating business and your personal life – and learning to stick with that.

There have been times – when I saw myself facing the jaws of that first huge bill, with no means of paying it; or as my mam sat there with her fingers glued together; or when I was crying alongside a colicky baby when I should have been preparing for a TV appearance – when I wondered if I really would make it. It is an accumulation of these choices, these lessons, that I have shared, that meant I was able to.

And if I can make it, so can you. We all can.

Acknowledgements

First of all, a huge thank-you to my parents for the love and support they have shown me my entire life – and my entire career! Your belief in me has been a huge part of my success . . . as was all the help with looking after the boys. I am truly grateful. Similarly, thank you to my in-laws, Val and John, for their constant support with everything, from day one. We'd all be lost without you!

Thank you also to the entire team at Crafter's Companion, who make the company what it is, and all of whom have had to sit through 'The Talk' over the years. For those of you who kept telling me to write a book – you see, I eventually listened!

As for the writing of the book, thank you to Alexandra Heminsley. I am a good storyteller but a terrible writer and you have helped me to find my voice on the page without compromising it, while being there for hours of laughter and tears along the way. And thank you to my publisher, Susanna Wadeson, and her team at Transworld, especially Katrina Whone, Sarah Day, Phil Lord, Cat Hillerton, Hayley Barnes, Sophie Bruce and all the sales team. And thank you to my agents Paul Stevens and Laura Hill at Independent Talent for introducing us all.

And I would not even be in this position if it wasn't for all of the crafters out there, who welcome me into their homes with such open hearts – albeit via the medium of TV and social media. You have been behind me since my very first product and it has been an honour to go on this crafting journey with you.

Finally, an enormous thank-you to Simon and our boys for giving up so much of our time together so that I could write this book. I was already so busy with work and dancing, but you still let me chip into family time so that I could really live out my dreams this last year. Here's to you living out yours next.

Sara Davies MBE is the youngest ever female investor to appear on BBC 1's *Dragon's Den* and is well-known as the founder and creative director of the global craft business, Crafter's Companion. Launched while she was still at university, Crafter's Companion is now a global business selling papercraft, art, needlecraft and stationery items across 40 countries with head offices in the US and UK. Sara lives with her husband and sons in Teeside.